Speaking Across the Curriculum

Practical Ideas for Incorporating Listening and Speaking into the Classroom

Speaking Across the Curriculum

*Practical Ideas for Incorporating Listening
and Speaking into the Classroom*

California High School Speech Association's Curriculum Committee

Speaking Across the Curriculum:
Practical Ideas for Incorporating Listening and Speaking into the Classroom

Published by
The International Debate Education Association
400 West 59th Street
New York, NY 10019

Activity sheets may be downloaded from www.idebate.org/speakingacross.htm

Library of Congress Cataloging-in-Publication Data

Speaking across the curriculum : practical ideas for incorporating
listening and speaking into the classroom.
        p. cm.
    Compiled by the California High School Speech Association's Curriculum Committee.
    Includes bibliographical references.
    ISBN 1-932716-00-9 (alk. paper)
    1. Debates and debating. 2. Public speaking. 3. Oral communication.
I. California High School Speech Association. Curriculum Committee.
PN4192.T43S64 2004
808.5'1--dc22   2004012506

Design by Kathleen Hayes
Printed in the USA

Preface

Public speaking is mandated as a required course by some high school districts; it is written into the English curriculum at other schools. Yet most of us realize that public speaking skills are not relegated to one or two subject areas outside of school.

Just as all professions encourage and reward effective communication skills, all courses—from algebra to history— benefit if students communicate effectively. If speaking and listening skills are expected and inspected by teachers across the curriculum, we stand to boost the level of critical thinking and analysis and to increase the level of discussion and discourse in all subject areas.

The materials in this book were designed to give teachers ready-made speaking and listening activities that could be infused into any curriculum. Assessment rubrics for individual speeches and group discussions have been included to make evaluating these skills more objective. For California teachers, all of the materials in this book are tied to the California English Language Arts Standards on our Web site, www.cahssa.org.

It is our hope that these materials will be useful in fostering the skills needed to communicate across the curriculum.

Lynette Williamson
Chair, California High School Speech Association's Curriculum Committee

Acknowledgments

The California High School Speech Association's Curriculum Committee compiled these materials from 1999–2003. The contributors listed below dedicated themselves to seeing this project through to its completion; many others offered what they could when they could; ALL were instrumental in making this project a success.

Neil Barembaum
Los Angeles Unified School District

Gay Brasher
San Jose Unified School District

John Cardoza
Carondelet High School, Concord

Donovan Cummings (retired)
Stockton Unified School District

Shirley Keller-Firestone (retired)
Fremont Union High School District

Karen Glahn-Meredith
Lincoln Unified School District

Andara Macdonald
Holtville Unified School District

Sharon Prefontaine
Fremont Union High School District

Rita Prichard
Roseville Joint Unified School District

Kate Shuster
Claremont McKenna College, Claremont Colleges' Debate Outreach

Janet Wilford
San Ramon Valley Unified School District

Lynette Williamson, chair
West Sonoma County Unified School District

Please Feed Us Back!
All of us on the curriculum committee have tested these ideas in our classrooms, yet these lessons remain "works in progress." We hope you will send us any comments or suggestions that you might have for making the materials more accessible either to you or to your students. You can reach us at www.cahssa.org.

Table of Contents

SECTION VII *Oral Interpretation*

SECTION VIII *Spontaneous Speaking*

APPENDIXES

SECTION I
Classroom Debate

Students love to argue. These classroom debate activities are designed to ensure that all students engaging in a classroom argument have the right to speak and be heard. Through these activities, students will be encouraged to argue ethically—supporting their claims with reason, evidence, and appropriate language.

"Yes, BUT . . . Yes, AND"

An efficient way to get all students discussing controversial topics.

Materials

None

Procedure

"Yes, BUT . . . "

1. Appoint or ask for a volunteer to present a controversial topic. The subject is the speaker's choice. The speaker goes to the front of the room and says, for example: " An abortion doctor was shot in front of a clinic last night. All protesters should be banned from picketing clinics." The speaker then calls on the people who want to oppose this view.

2. A respondent raises his/her hand and, after being called upon, replies, "Yes, but . . . " and presents his/her opposing view.

3. The person usually stands by his/her desk.

4. The speaker then calls on the next student to respond to the previous student, and so on until all opposing points are brought out.

5. Once an issue is exhausted, the speaker reclaims his/her seat, and another student takes over the activity by introducing another subject.

"Yes, AND . . . "

1. Eventually, students will realize that all of the opposing arguments have been given, and they want to add something to emphasize one side or the other. When they ask how to do this, suggest that they say: "yes, and . . . " and then continue to give information that will reinforce the argument. ("Yes, and . . . " is also a good tool to use when the topic is informational.)

2. The discussion can go on for as long as you wish. It usually works best, however, if you limit the time to 15–20 minutes. It works well either on Mondays to get the week going, or on Fridays for a wrap-up.

3. You might want to require students to bring in newspapers or magazine articles so they can introduce more current, viable information into the discussion.

Teacher Tips

1. This exercise works best if you first explain it to the class and then carefully model the first example.

2. You may have to regulate how many times a person can respond to a statement to avoid having one person monopolize the activity.

Evaluation

1. You can assign as many participation points as you like for each speaker's efforts.

2. You may want to consider the following criteria for awarding credit:
   - contributed a pertinent comment
   - added something new to the discussion
   - clashed with opponent(s) in "Yes, but . . . "

Dialogue

A cooperative activity that shares ideas and knowledge
for the benefit of two speakers and the members of the audience.

Materials
Sample "Pre-think" for Literature Dialogues
Dialogue Scoring Guide
Listening Rubric (page 142)

Procedure
You can approach this activity in two ways: (a) The dialogue may be spontaneous, in which case it will contain generalizations and personal opinions, but may elicit more honest, immediate responses (gut-reaction). Or (b) The dialogue many be based on a "pre-think" (assigned) topic. This type of dialogue may encourage more analysis and reflective thinking, but may also prompt more artificial responses. If you are using this type of dialogue, you might require students to include quoted material from references or works studied or read. (See Sample "Pre-think" for Literature Dialogues for sample questions.)

1. Create a number of expository questions based on specific information, an issue, a concept, or a literary theme. For example:
   a. **specific information:** To what extent can the media be held responsible for violence in America?
   b. **an issue:** Should society's fear of the use of certain scientific research prevent that research from being pursued?
   c. **a concept:** Can socialism or capitalism better meet the economic needs of a country?
   d. **literary theme:** The concept of evil dominates in *Frankenstein, Heart of Darkness, East of Eden, Lord of the Flies,* and *Bless Me, Ultima.* Is evil relative or absolute?
2. Write each question on a single piece of paper and place in a bowl or box.
3. Distribute and review the Dialogue Scoring Guide.
4. Select two students at random to form a team and have the team draw a question.
5. Give each team a maximum of 2 minutes to brainstorm ideas on the question. Team members must not discuss the question during this time.
6. Give each team 5 minutes for a dialogue. Remind the team members that they are responsible for making sure that the dialogue is balanced—featuring both speakers.

Teacher Tips
How do you keep the other students engaged while teams are dialoguing? Try one of the following strategies:
1. Divide the students into small groups. Have them control preparation and speaking time, and allow them to score each other using the "Dialogue" evaluation form. (They may be more critical than you would be.)
2. Tell the class that each time a dialogue is finished, you will randomly select a student to briefly outline the key points made in the course of the conversation. He/she can do this from memory or notes.
3. Tell the students you will grade them on their listening. The Listening Rubric is a helpful "threat" anytime you need a cooperative audience. Distribute the rubric to the students and let them know that they are being graded on these skills,

Evaluation
You can use the Dialogue Scoring Guide to assess the teams. Alternately, you can ask the students in the audience to use the form to judge the dialogue.

Sample "Pre-Think" for Literature Dialogues

Here is an example of an inventory discussing the theme of "evil" in literature. Dialogue teams could use the following questions as topics.

Evil Inventory

Before we begin [name of novel or literary work], it's important for you to articulate your own thoughts on the concept of evil. Please answer the following questions thoughtfully. You will be using this sheet in conjunction with other materials to prepare for a dialogue.

1. What does the word evil mean? (You may want to skip this question and answer it after you've considered the other ones.)

2. Is there absolute evil, or does evil depend on circumstances?

3. Do you agree or disagree that most people are fascinated with evil? Support your answer with an example; then speculate as to why or why not.

4. Should society be protected from evil people? Why or why not?

5. Are there ever any circumstances that warrant protecting an evil person from society? Explain.

6. Can an entire society be evil to the extent that the violation of human rights is accepted as moral and just?

7. Does evil exist independently of good, or can evil be defined only on the basis of what it is not?

8. Are all people capable of evil? Explain.

9. What role does personal restraint play in evil acts?

Dialogue Scoring Guide

Dialoguers:_____ & _____

Question:_____

	Superior	Excellent	Good	OK	Ooops!	Comments
Thoughtful Reflection The deeper you go into the complexity of the topic, the better.	5	4	3	2	1	
Use of Specific Examples Tag the text! The more examples you use from the novel, the articles read, current events and even personal anecdotes—the better! Avoid sweeping generalizations, e.g., "Athletes have all the advantages in school."	5	4	3	2	1	
Cooperation Encourage each other! Students may disagree, but shouldn't reject the other person's opinion. Students lose points for being antagonistic or critical (a.k.a. nasty). Strive to share the time equally.	5	4	3	2	1	
Usage and Grammar Beware of informal usage. Try to avoid the words "you" and "thing." Speak in complete sentences.	5	4	3	2	1	

Total Points_____

Four-Step Refutation

An exercise in clash.

Materials

Four-Step Refutation Summary
Hat or other receptacle (optional)

Procedure

1. Teach students the Four-Step Refutation, using the Four-Step Refutation Summary.
2. Have the students form two single-file lines, facing the front of the classroom. The student at the front of the left line should begin the game by making a claim—any claim, such as "Schools should not serve junk food" or "Jazz is the best kind of music."
3. The student at the front of the right line must refute the argument, using the four-step method.
4. When finished, these two students go to the back of the opposite line. The exercise repeats, until all students have made a claim and refuted a claim.

Teacher Tips

Variations

1. You can vary this game by passing around the "argument hat," a receptacle filled with small slips of paper on which you or the students have written simple claims about a variety of topics. Students draw an argument, read it aloud, and then refute it, using the four-step method.
2. Have students write a separate response for each of the "therefore examples" described under step 4 of the Four-Step Refutation Summary.

Evaluation

Ask all students to write a self-evaluation of the exercise and determine goals for future argumentation.

Four-Step Refutation Summary

Debates require clash. Clash happens in a debate when one speaker directly answers, or *refutes*, an argument that has been advanced by another speaker. Debates can't be composed of unrelated claims, like this example:

Speaker 1: *Bananas are better than apples because they contain more potassium.*
Speaker 2: *Circles are better than squares because their shape is more pleasing to the eye.*

In this example, both speakers are making arguments, but there is no actual debate happening because there is no refutation.

One of the most effective ways of refuting an argument is to use the Four-Step Refutation, summarized below

Step 1: "They say . . ."

It is important to reference the argument you are about to refute so that your audience can easily follow your line of thought. Unlike the bananas/oranges example, debates contain many different arguments. Unless you directly reference the arguments you are dealing with, you risk confusing the audience. Good note-taking skills will help you track individual arguments and how they have been refuted.

Remember to reference rather than repeat your opponent's argument. If you were to repeat all of your opponent's arguments, you wouldn't have any speech time to advance arguments of your own. Additionally, you risk reinforcing your opponent's argument by better explaining it. So try to rephrase the argument that you're about to refute in just three to seven words: "They say Batman is better than Superman, but . . ."

Step 2: "But I disagree . . ."

In this part of your refutation, you state the basics of your counter-argument. This can be, as in the case of the banana-orange controversy, simply the opposite of your opponent's claim. It can also be an attack on your opponent's reasoning or evidence. The important thing is to state clearly and concisely the counter-argument you want the judge to endorse.

Step 3: "Because . . ."

Having advanced your counter-argument, you need to proceed to offer reasoning. Your reasoning can be independent support for your counter-claim, as in the case above. It can also be a reasoned criticism of the opponent's argument.

Step 4: "Therefore . . ."

Finally, you need to draw a conclusion that compares your refutation to your opponents' argument and shows why yours defeats theirs. This conclusion is usually done by means of comparison, either of reasons or evidence or both. You need to show that your argument is better than their argument because it is:

- **Better reasoned.** Perhaps their argument makes some kind of error in logic or reasoning, of the kind discussed in "Logical Fallacies" (pp. 21–23).
- **Better evidenced.** Maybe your argument makes use of more or better evidence. Perhaps your sources are better qualified than theirs, or your evidence is more recent than theirs.
- **Empirical.** When we say that an argument is empirically proven, we mean that it is demonstrated by past examples. Perhaps your argument relies on empirics, while theirs relies on speculation.
- **Takes theirs into account.** Sometimes your argument may take theirs into account and go a step further. "Even if they're right about the recreational benefits of crossbows, they're still too dangerous for elementary school physical education classes."
- **Has a greater expressed significance.** You can state that your argument has more significance than your opponents' argument because (for example) it matters more to any given individual or applies more to a larger number of individuals.
- **Consistent with experience.** Perhaps your argument is consistent with experience over time, in a different place, or in different circumstances.

If the speakers above used the four-step refutation, their debate would be:

Speaker 1: *Bananas are better than oranges because they contain more potassium.*
Speaker 2: *Speaker 1 says that bananas are better than oranges, but I disagree. Oranges are better than bananas because they contain more vitamin C. Therefore, you should prefer oranges because while many foods in an ordinary diet contain potassium, few contain an appreciable amount of vitamin C. It is more important to eat oranges whenever possible than it is to eat bananas.*

Logical Fallacies

Watch for these tricks of argumentation!

Materials

Listening for Faulty Reasoning/Logical Fallacies
Fallacy Fix-it Worksheet

Procedure

1. Use the Listening for Faulty Reasoning/Logical Fallacies to teach students how to recognize logical fallacies.
2. Ask the students to complete the Fallacy Fix-it Worksheet and review it in class to make sure they understand logical fallacies.
3. Ask students to search popular magazines to find advertisements that use one or more logical fallacies.
4. Tell the students to cut out the advertisements and create a visual to present to the class, explaining how each advertisement uses faulty reasoning.

Teacher Tips

1. You can use this procedure to analyze any number of argumentative materials such as: advertising, political speeches, editorials, political debates, or promotional materials.
2. Students could work in groups to analyze the argumentative material and present their findings to the class.

Evaluation

Ask students to hand in a written analysis of the magazine advertisement, their Fallacy Fix-it Worksheets, or other analysis of fallacious arguments.

Listening for Faulty Reasoning/Logical Fallacies

One of the most important skills you must learn in debate is how to listen. A good listener analyzes what he hears. Listeners who believe everything they are told can get into a lot of trouble. Be especially alert when listening to messages that are meant to persuade you. Be prepared to catch the speaker who has not constructed an argument using sound reasoning but depends, instead, on misleading you.

Logical fallacies are forms of arguments that are not acceptable because they contain a flaw in reasoning. Recognize these!

I. Fallacies of Whiles and Parts

A. *Fallacy of composition*: What is true of the parts is also true of the whole. "My grandmother is a horrible driver so I don't trust riding with old people. They are very dangerous and should have their licenses taken away!"

B. *Fallacy of division*: What is true of the whole is true of each part. "All birds have wings. Wings serve the function of flight. So all birds fly."

II. Fallacies of Causation

A. *Fallacy of mistaken causation*: Mistaking a symptom or sign for a cause. "All week I have been so thirsty! I know I must have diabetes!"

B. *Post hoc ergo propter hoc*: After the fact, therefore because of the fact. "History tells us that Jimmy Carter, a Democrat, was not a strong president. Democrat Bill Clinton's presidency was fraught with controversy. Future Democratic presidents will surely be weak leaders."

C. *Slippery Slope*: Claims that an event will set off an uncontrollable chain reaction when there is no real reason to expect that reaction to occur. "If we start regulating carbon dioxide, the next thing you know politicians will be telling you what to eat for breakfast."

III. Fallacies in Using Numbers

A. *Fallacy of significance*: Citing statistics without the necessary context or clarification. "Abortion should be illegal because 99% are done for convenience. Only 1% are performed because of incest or rape." How many abortions are done each year? How many abortions constitute 1% of the 1.2 million abortions each year? Have you done the math? Is this really an insignificant number?

B. *Argumentum ad populum* (Bandwagon): Appeal to popular opinion when the speaker asks the listener to become part of a supposedly overwhelming group in favor of some person, product, or idea. "Prior to the Civil War, slavery was just and necessary in the South because the majority of the people wanted it." Is something moral just because the majority votes for it?

IV. False Dilemma

Suggesting a limited number of choices. "Deciding the issue of capital punishment is simple; either we have it or we don't." There are actually many choices we can make in the way we deal with serious crimes. What about life in prison, work/restitution, torture, rehabilitation, etc.?

V. Loaded Language (Fallacy of Psychological Language)

A. *Labels*: Using a label to arouse the audience's emotions. "Racist comments, 'Read my Lips,' KKK, Nazi Germany, Hitler . . . "

B. *Stereotypes*: Suggesting that one example holds true for all cases. "The most violent gangs are Asian gangs."

C. *Loaded question or statement*: Asking an unfair question where any answer will condemn the speaker. "Do you think you are smarter than most of your friends?" A "yes," even if it is true, may make you feel egotistical. A "no" may make you appear untruthful, when you get the best grades.

D. *Grandstanding*: Appealing to popular sentiment or prejudice. Changing a position for the purpose of gaining votes or favor.

VI. Ignoring the Issue

A. *Red herring*: Raising an irrelevant issue. "When President George H.W. Bush became physically ill at the table at the summit with Japan, he ruined any chances of successful negotiations."

B. *Smokescreen*: Clouding the issue. "I have just described every detail of my Aunt Gladys' terminal illness. She suffered tremendously. These heartbreaking events should convince you to make physician-assisted mercy killing legal."

C. *Tu quoque*: Defending one's actions by charging the opponent with the same behavior. "I wasn't the only one who took campaign contributions from lobbyists. My opponent did the same."

D. *Straw man*: Refuting only the weaker arguments of the opposition. "Yes we can discuss the economy, education, and foreign policy. Let's begin by questioning my opponent's use of a limousine to get here today."

E. *Ad hominem*: Attacks on the opposing speaker's character, rather than the ideas presented. "You notice that my opponent's answer to that reporter's question about the Japanese Trade Agreement was rude and insulting. Can we believe a candidate who shows such rudeness to the free press?"

VII. Fallacies in Using Evidence

A. *Quoting out of context*: Misrepresenting the author's opinion. Using only part of a quote or changing words for the purpose of leading the listener to believe certain things.

B. *Hasty generalizations*: Basing a generalization on cases that are unrepresentative or insufficient in number. "The states of Montana, Ohio, Oklahoma, North Dakota, South Dakota and Kansas are free of pollution. Why does the United States need a federal smog emission law?"

C. *Weak analogy*: An argument's conclusion rests on a nonexistent similarity between two examples: "Well, if it worked in a college term paper, it'll work in American foreign policy."

VIII. Scare Tactics

Using the threat of harm to advance the conclusion. "Who knows what hidden dangers still lie in the storage areas of the Rancho Seco Nuclear Power Plant, closed in the 1980s. Nuclear waste presents a danger to you and your family! That is why I urge you to have it remain closed. Do you want to die?"

IX. Appeal to Ignorance

Suggesting that the opponent's inability to disprove a conclusion actually proves the conclusion correct. "I haven't heard my opponent prove his points very well, so you have no choice but to implement mine."

Fallacy Fix-it Worksheet

Each of the following arguments uses at least one logical fallacy. Identify why each argument is fallacious and improve it by re-wording.

1. Every atom in my body is invisible. Therefore, I am invisible.

2. If you want to grow up to be like Wonder Woman, you'd better eat those carrots.

3. Where did you hide the cookies you stole?

4. Songwriter Elton John says Sinclair Paints are the best. So be sure to use Sinclair Paints when you redecorate your home.

5. Philosophers are highly intelligent individuals, because if they weren't highly intelligent, they wouldn't be philosophers.

6. Ronald Reagan met with space aliens in 1987, and that cannot be disproved.

7. Sodium and chlorine, the atomic components of salt, are deadly poisons. Therefore, salt is a deadly poison.

Taking Notes in Debate: Fun With Lists

An exercise to improve debate skills by listening and writing quickly.

Materials

None

Procedure

1. Have students prepare to take notes. Explain that you will read a series of lists to them and that they should try to write down as many of the list items as they can.

2. Begin with the simpler lists on the left, and proceed to the more complex lists on the right. After each list, stop and ask students to repeat the items on the list in order.

List 1	List 2	List 3	List 4	List 5
5	Toyota	Orange	Tom Brokaw	George Bush
64	Honda	Suburban	Diane Sawyer	Volvo
578	Kia	12	Dan Rather	27
2	Ferrari	Friends	Peter Jennings	Cabbage
99	Mitsubishi	Internet	Regis Philbin	Halloween
1,023	Chevrolet	56	Bill O'Reilly	Cheerios
73	Mercedes-Benz	Acura	Leslie Stahl	882
5,598	Ford	Yellow	Wolf Blitzer	Rottweiler
	Cadillac			Eagle

Teacher Tips

1. Gradually increase your speed as you progress from list to list. Develop lists of your own, with more diverse and longer content. You might prepare lists of assertions on a given topic and have students write down all of the assertions in order. This will help them prepare for taking notes in a debate. For example, you might read the following list to students, saying the letters out loud:

• Education policy should be reformed.
• There are no problems in our schools today.
• Students have too much homework.
• Teachers really care about students.
• Schools should require students to learn a foreign language.

These sorts of lists are helpful as teaching tools because you can ask students to show which of the statements contradict each other and how the statements could be revised to make them consistent.

2. You can also ask students to make each assertion into a complete argument.

Taking Notes in Debate: Now You're Cooking!

An exercise to develop the debate skill of taking notes on unfamiliar information.

Materials

One or more cookbooks, preferably books that contain recipes using ingredients with which the students will not be familiar. Scan the books ahead of time to identify a few recipes that you will read to the students.

Procedure

1. Have the students prepare to take notes. Explain that you will be reading them a recipe and that they should try to write down all of the ingredients.
2. Read the students your chosen recipe or the recipe below.

   ### Aloo-Gosht
   Ingredients
   1 kilo lamb/goat/beef meat
   500 gm small potatoes
   1 large onion thinly sliced
   75 gm natural yogurt
   2 teaspoons coriander powder
   1 teaspoon cumin
   1½ teaspoon chili powder
   150 gm ghee or oil
   2 teaspoons ginger paste
   2 teaspoons garlic paste
   1 bay leaf
   1 teaspoon turmeric
   garam masala made of
      3 black cardamom
      1 inch cinnamon
      4 cloves
      5 green cardamom
      12 black peppercorns
   1 or 2 teaspoons salt

Teacher Tips

After you read the recipe, have the students read their lists aloud. Keep track of their mistakes without correcting their presentations. After all students have presented their lists, read the correct list. You might want to announce the name of the student whose list was closest to the original.

Taking Notes in Debate: Playing Cards

An exercise using playing cards to teach students how to flow in debates.

Materials

deck of standard playing cards
Flowing Summary
Sample Flow Sheet

Procedure

1. Use Flowing Summary to discuss and review flowing.
2. Give each student a copy of the Sample Flow Sheet and ask an experienced student to serve as scribe during the activity.
3. Shuffle a standard deck of cards.
4. Explain to the students that you will begin with the arguments made by an imaginary first speaker for the proposing side. The students should write down each argument, which will be represented by a playing card. Emphasize to the students that they must space out the individual arguments on their page, leaving space between each argument so they can effectively track the responses.
5. Begin with the first speaker's arguments. Pull four cards from the deck and number them, i.e., "My first argument is the Jack of Hearts. My second argument is the Four of Spades. My third argument is the Seven of Diamonds. My fourth argument is the King of Diamonds." Many students will not use appropriate abbreviations for these first cards, so you might want to go over the flow sheet to make sure students are using an effective abbreviation system.
6. Next deliver the first opposing speaker's arguments. Be creative, and make sure you use relational references to illustrate the clash of arguments. As students get more advanced, you can increase your use of the terms used in formal debates. Here's an example speech and the corresponding flow sheet:

> *"They say 'Jack of Hearts.' First, that's not true because of the Eight of Clubs. Second, Queen of Diamonds. Now, they say 'Four of Spades.' My first answer is Two of Hearts. Second, the Ace of Spades disproves that argument. Their third argument is the Seven of Diamonds. However, this Seven of Diamonds argument proves our side. Also, Nine of Hearts. Their final argument is the King of Diamonds. But I've already answered this with the Queen of Diamonds. Second, Five of Diamonds. Third, Two of Spades."*

First Proposing	First Opposing	Second Proposing	Second Opposing
1. JH ⟶	1. Not true: 8C 2. QD		
2. 4S ⟶	1. 2H 2. AS disproves		
3. 7D ⟶	1. 7D proves our side 2. 9H		
4. KD ⟶	1. Ans. by QD 2. 5D 3. 2S		

Many of the students will be lost at this point, so you should have your scribe (or you) read over the master flow sheet so students can make corrections to their flow sheets. Then you can deliver the third speech to demonstrate how argument extension works. Here's another sample speech and the corresponding flow sheet:

> "Extend our first argument, the Jack of Hearts. First, the Eight of Clubs contradicts the Queen of Diamonds. Second, Four of Clubs. Now, on our second argument, we said Four of Spades. They say Two of Hearts and Ace of Spades, but the Four of Spades is more recent than the Two of Hearts. Also, there's no evidence for the Ace of Spades. On our third point, we said Seven of Diamonds. They said this proves their side, but they're wrong—it proves our side because Ace of Diamonds. Finally, extend our argument about the King of Diamonds. This is more important than their point. Also, the Five of Diamonds and the Two of Spades are empirically wrong. The Seven of Clubs proves this."

First Proposing	First Opposing	Second Proposing	Second Opposing
1. JH	1. Not true: 8C 2. QD	Extend JH. 1. 8C contradicts QD. 2. 4C	
2. 4S	1. 2H 2. AS disproves	1. 4S is more recent than 2H. 2. no ev for AS.	
3. 7D	1. 7D proves our side 2. 9H	7D actually proves our side: AD.	
4. KD	1. Ans. By QD 2. 5D 3. 2S	1. Extend KD. Outweighs theirs. 2. 5D and 2S empirically wrong: 7C.	

7. You can continue the exercise, but this is usually enough for beginning students. Explain to students that this process shows how arguments are made and relate to each other in debates. Tell them that the cards only represent arguments, and in debates they will have to track real arguments and how they relate to each other.

Flowing Summary

Good note-taking abilities are essential for success in debate. If you are able to track how arguments relate to each other, you will be able to compare and contrast the balance of arguments.

The system used to take notes in a debate is called "flowing." It's called flowing because arguments flow across the page as they relate to each other. Taking notes in this format provides a map of the debate and shows what was said and by whom. Flowing also allows you to plan specific attacks on your opponent's arguments, and organizes your thoughts for your speeches. You make a flow by taking notes of each speech in a column.

Do not try to write down every word your opponent says. Try to capture only the major ideas and arguments of your opponent. It will be important to use symbols and abbreviations to help you take more efficient notes.

Normally, there are two sides in a debate. One side makes a case for the motion for debate (they *propose* the motion, for example), while the other side argues against that case (they *oppose* the motion). The two sides alternate speeches as the debate progresses. This process is graphically represented in a debater's notes. Here's an example of a bad debate:

Proposing side	Opposing Side	Proposing Side	Opposing Side	Proposing Side
Yes ⟶	No ⟶	Yes ⟶	No ⟶	Yes

Why is this an example of a bad debate? The example "debaters" are not making arguments, and just saying "Yes" and "No." In this sample of note taking, you can see that arrows are used to show how arguments relate to each other in a debate.

Practical Hints for Flowing
- Shorten each word to 1–2 syllables.
- Eliminate vowels when abbreviating.
- Use the minimum number of notations, but make sure you can understand what you have written.
- Use lines and arrows to connect arguments for both debaters.

Sample Flow Sheet

Using the Sample Flowsheet

Below, you will find a sample flowsheet that represents notes for part of a debate on the topic "Schools should require student uniforms." One team proposes the topic. This team makes a brief case for student uniforms. They advance three basic arguments:

- Cost. Many students can't afford to look sharp every day for school, and students get embarrassed if they don't have the latest fashions.
- Uniforms aren't as distracting, and will help students focus on their classwork, not their clothes.
- Uniforms reduce violence, because students can't wear gang clothes or gang symbols.

Then the first opposition speaker refutes the case. She might begin by bringing up the issue of freedom of expression. She could say that uniforms are a bad idea because students need to be able to express their individuality in school. Then she would move on to answer the arguments made in the proposition's case. On the "cost" point, she might say that uniforms are expensive, too, particularly since people have to buy a bunch of them at once. On the "distraction" point, she could say that there are always things to distract students, and that districts have dress codes in place to deal with distracting clothing. Finally, on the "violence" point, she could say that dress codes already prevent gang clothing, and that uniforms won't reduce the gang problem because students who want to be in gangs will be in them whether or not they have to wear uniforms.

Then the second proposition speaker has to answer the opposition's arguments while rebuilding and extending on the proposition's case. The flowsheet will help her do this, as she knows what arguments she has to answer and extend upon. She should begin by answering the freedom of expression argument by saying, for example, that students have many ways to express themselves, and that clothes are a shallow and unimportant method of expression. Then she can move on to rebuild her team's case. To extend on the "cost" argument, she should probably reiterate it briefly before beginning her refutation: "We said that many students can't afford to keep up with the latest trends, and that's embarrassing. Now, they say that uniforms are expensive to buy, but they're cheap compared to the latest pair of Nikes or Hilfigers, and that means that poorer students won't be made fun of for their clothes." She could repeat this process by moving through the other opposition arguments and rebuilding her case.

First Proposing	First Opposing	Second Proposing	Second Opposing
Students should have uniforms.	Hurts freedom of expression— students need to express individuality. →	1. Students have other ways to express themselves. 2. Clothes not important for expression— too shallow.	
1. Cost—many can't afford expensive clothes; are embarrassed. →	Uniforms expensive too— must buy a lot at once. →	Students can't keep up with trends—Nikes. Even if uniforms expensive, clothes are worse. Also, poor students won't be made fun of.	
2. Not as distracting, so students can focus on classwork. →	1. Always things to distract students. 2. Dress codes address the problem.		
3. Reduce violence— students can't wear gang symbols or clothes. →	1. Dress codes already stop gang clothing. 2. Uniforms won't help—they join for other reasons.		

Spontaneous Argumentation (SpAr)

Spontaneous Argumentation is a mini-debate. You can use SpAr
to have the students discuss propositions derived from the curriculum.

Materials

Silly SpAr Topics
SpAr Evaluation Form
Appendix 7: Warm Up Exercises (optional)

Procedure

1. Select a topic drawn from classroom instruction. It should be a statement with which reasonable people may agree or disagree. Topics should *not* be questions. For example:
   - **Art:** Resolved: There is an objective way to determine what is art.
   - **Biology:** Resolved: A person's genetic makeup determines who he or she is.
   - **English:** Resolved: Owen Meany should have avoided his destiny, not embraced it.
   - **Math (Integrated):** Resolved: Tables convey better information than graphs.
   - **Physical Education:** Resolved: Perfecting your best skills is more effective than improving your weak ones.

   If this is your first experiment with SpAr, you may want to use one of the silly SpAr topics from the list that follows this activity. Students can practice SpAr format without worrying about the weight of their arguments.
2. Select two students who will speak from the front of the room. Assign one student to debate the Affirmative, supporting the topic, and the other student the Negative, opposing the topic. If the speakers need invigorating, employ the warm up exercises from Appendix 7.
3. Give the students the topic and explain the criteria for evaluation (below).
4. Ask the students to look at the topic for 1 minute. The debate progresses using the following format:

Affirmative Opening	1 minute
Negative Opening	1 minute
Unstructured Argumentation*	3 minutes
Negative Closing	1 minute
Affirmative Closing	1 minute

*In "Unstructured Argumentation" each student should be
polite but firm in asserting his/her right to speak, while allowing
his/her opponent a chance to speak.

5. You may need to clarify the speakers' duties. One-minute speeches may not lend themselves to highly structured organizational schemes. Nevertheless, they should still give a sense of having a beginning, a middle, and an end. There should be an introductory remark or two, a brief presentation of arguments supporting the assigned position, and some concluding remarks. All speeches other than the first affirmative should make some reference to what was said previously.
6. Students do not address each other during speeches: They address the audience. Students may address each other during the unstructured argumentation, but they still face the audience, not each other.

Evaluation

Each student is judged individually on his or her performance. This is *not* a win-lose debate. You can use the SpAr Evaluation Form to evaluate students on the following:

- **Use of information:** Although this is an "unprepared" activity, the student should be able to use course content to support his position. This criterion can involve demonstrating a certain required amount of knowledge, and also the ability to adapt information to advance a position.
- **Analysis:** Students need to use logic and reasoning, critical thinking, and clear argumentation.
- **Clash:** Students are expected to respond to each other's arguments. The activity is not simply "impromptu for two"—two ships that pass in the night. Each volley of argument should advance the debate. The closing speeches should reflect some progress in treating the topic, not just a repetition of the opening statement.
- **Etiquette:** The speakers should listen attentively while an opponent is speaking. During Unstructured Argumentation, students should be polite, allowing their opponent to speak, but they need to assert their right to speak. Students should be aggressive, but you should discourage a free-for-all simultaneous argument.

Silly SpAr Topics

Animals are appropriate mascots for high schools.

Backpacks are better than lockers.

Barbie is a more appropriate role model than GI Joe.

Belts are preferable to suspenders.

Blondes have more fun.

Bowling should be the national sport of the United States.

Breakfast is the most important meal of the day.

Buttons are better than zippers.

Cats are better pets than dogs.

Children watch too much TV.

Cows are better than horses.

Dark chocolate is better than white chocolate.

Disneyland represents all that is best about America.

Doritos are better than Pringles.

Football is the most violent sport.

Halloween is a better holiday than Valentine's Day.

Make up should be banned from high schools.

Penmanship should be a required subject in high school.

Rock is better than Rap.

Santa is better than the Easter Bunny.

Showers are better than baths.

Sleep is for wimps.

Softball is easier to play than hardball.

Sunday is the worst day for watching TV.

There should be a single presidential term of six years.

SpAr Evaluation Form

Names (Aff)_____ vs. (Neg) _____

	Knock Out	Won on Points	Draw	Sucker Punch
Affirmative				
Use of information	5	4	3	2 / 1
Analysis	5	4	3	2 / 1
Clash	5	4	3	2 / 1
Etiquette	5	4	3	2 / 1
Negative				
Use of information	5	4	3	2 / 1
Analysis	5	4	3	2 / 1
Clash	5	4	3	2 / 1
Etiquette	5	4	3	2 / 1

Panel Debate

Students will participate in a panel debate on a controversial issue and interact with the class during question/answer segments.

Materials

Appendix 1: How to Select a Topic
Debate Duties and Procedures
Appendix 3: Constructing a Speech for Debate
Panel Debate Critiques
Appendix 7: Warm Up Exercises (optional)

Procedure

1. Select a topic and present it in a resolution format (see Appendix 1: How to Select a Topic). Topics should be controversial, balanced, a statement made in positive form (avoiding "not"). Keep the wording simple and clear.

2. Determine who will be moderator; who will present the affirmative arguments; and who will present the negative arguments. Give the participants copies of Debate Duties and Procedures to prepare them for the formal debate.

3. Tell the panel to begin research using the following rules. (You may want to give the panel a print copy of the rules for reference.)

   • Each member of the panel is responsible for three sources of information on the topic. Only one of these may be exclusively from the Internet.

   • Each piece of research must be clearly labeled with the following source information: author, title of source, date of publication, and page numbers.

   • Each member must be prepared to share his/her research with his/her panel members on both the Affirmative and the Negative.

   It's helpful if each student highlights or brackets key arguments and evidence in the information they've researched. (For tips on constructing speeches, see Appendix 3: Constructing a Speech for Debate.)

Evaluation

Use Panel Debate Critiques to evaluate the debate.

Debate Duties and Procedures

The Moderator

Beginning of the debate: the moderator introduces the topic, defines the terms, and gives background information. For example: if the topic were capital punishment, the moderator might give a brief history of capital punishment in the United States, define capital punishment, and summarize current law.

The debaters need to know the content of this introduction prior to the presentation.

During the debate: the moderator introduces the debaters and keeps track of time

At the conclusion of each debater's speech: the moderator calls on opposing debaters and/or class members to ask questions of the speakers (if needed, the moderator may ask questions).

At the conclusion of the debate: the moderator offers a 1–3 minute summary of the main issues presented by each side in the debate

The Debaters

The presentation of the arguments and evidence should be equally divided between the team members. Each debater is expected to ask questions of the opposition (see Appendix 2: How to Ask Questions in a Debate). If the speakers need invigorating, employ the warm up exercises from Appendix 7.

The First Affirmative Speaker's 2–5 minute speech will include:
- at least two arguments in favor of the resolution
- evidence from the research that supports the arguments

The first affirmative's opening speech will be fully prepared before the debate

The First Negative Speaker's 2–5 minute speech will include:
- at least two arguments against the resolution
- evidence from the research that supports the arguments
- refutation of the affirmative speaker's arguments (see Four-Step Refutation Summary, pp. 18–19)

The Second Affirmative Speaker's 2–5 minute speech will include:
- at least one new argument in favor of the resolution
- evidence from the research that supports the arguments
- refutation of the negative speaker's arguments (see Four-Step Refutation Summary)

The Second Negative Speaker's 2–5 minute speech will include:

- at least one new argument against the resolution
- evidence from the research that supports the arguments
- refutation of the affirmative speakers' arguments (see Four-Step Refutation Summary)
- a final statement of the negative position

The First Affirmative Speaker's 1–2 minute speech will include:

- refutation of the negative speakers' arguments (see Four-Step Refutation Summary)
- a final statement of the affirmative position

The Audience

Class members *are expected to:*

- take notes
- ask pertinent questions of the debaters during allotted questioning

Class members *may:*

- be asked to write a brief comment on their personal attitude toward the topic prior to the debate
- be asked to indicate any change in their opinion and why
- be asked to write an evaluation of the debate.

The debate will be conducted on the following time schedule:

Moderator Intro	2–3 minutes
First Affirmative Speaker	2–5 minutes
Questions	1–3 minutes
First Negative Speaker	2–5 minutes
Questions	1–3 minutes
Second Affirmative Speaker	2–5 minutes
Questions	1–3 minutes
Second Negative Speaker	2–5 minutes
Questions	1–3 minutes
First Affirmative Speaker	1–2 minutes
Moderator Summary	1–3 minutes

Panel Debate Critiques

Moderator

Name_____Topic _____

	Beyond the Call of Duty	Impres- sive!	Good	So-So	Huh?	Comments
Opening Speech: balance of presentation, organization, research (min. 3 sources)	5	4	3	2	I	
Moderation of Panel	5	4	3	2	I	
Summary Statement	5	4	3	2	I	

Panelist

Name_____Topic _____

	Beyond the Call of Duty	Impres- sive!	Good	So-So	Huh?	Comments
Opening Speech: balance of presentation, organization, research (min. 3 sources)	5	4	3	2	I	
Moderation of Panel	5	4	3	2	I	
Summary Statement	5	4	3	2	I	

Classroom Congress

A chance to discuss contemporary issues in sessions that encourage critical thinking and a tolerance of different viewpoints.

Materials

Appendix 1: How to Select a Topic for Debate
Bills and Resolutions
Congress Conventions
Appendix 2: How to Ask Questions in a Debate
Classroom Congress Critique
Appendix 7: Warm Up Exercises (optional)

Procedure

1. Select a topic and present it in a resolution format (see Appendix 1: How to Select a Topic for Debate). Topics should be controversial, balanced, a statement made in positive form (avoiding "not"). Keep the wording simple and clear.

2. Select the presiding officer (PO), or you may assume the role. This individual serves as a moderator, recognizing speakers and questioners and maintaining order through parliamentary procedure. The PO gives appropriate time signals, establishes a tone of formality, and prevents flippant, off-hand remarks or personal attacks.

3. Select two students to support the resolution and two students to oppose the resolution each week. Each member of the class should have a chance to present a formal argument for or against a particular piece of legislation during the semester. Any other members of the class can offer additional speeches in support or opposition to the legislation at any time.

4. Set up the Session:

   a. Give the students copies of Bills and Resolutions and explain the characteristics of each type of legislation.

   b. Provide students with specific legislation or divide students into committees to brainstorm topics and write their own bills and resolutions.

   c. Provide an opportunity for peer editing and small-group revision.

   d. Type, duplicate, and distribute the legislation.

   e. Have the entire class set the order in which the legislation will be discussed.

   f. Brief the legislation:
   - Terms to define
   - Research options
   - Pertinent historical information
   - Anticipated arguments

   g. Assign research for each small group, giving students time to build arguments and select support materials.

   h. Pass out Congress Conventions and review basic parliamentary procedure.

   i. Present the requirements for the session:
   - Deliver arguments from the front of the room.
   - Begin with a salutation "Members of the House . . ."
   - Take notes to support the eventual written vote.

- Direct all comments toward the speaker or presiding officer.
- Speak only when called upon by the presiding officer.

5. If the speakers need invigorating, employ the warm up exercises from Appendix 7.

6. Conduct the Session:

   a. Call session to order, reinforcing the basic rules of conduct and courtesy.

   b. Read or ask that the legislation be read.

   c. Call on one of the assigned affirmative speakers or ask for an affirmative volunteer.

   d. Open the cross-examination period when the speaker concludes. (See Appendix 2: How to Ask Questions in a Debate.) Encourage all students to ask questions they deem relevant. Limit questions to one sentence.

   e. Call on one of the assigned negative speakers or ask for a negative volunteer.

   f. Open the cross-examination period when speaker concludes.

   g. Alternate in the same manner, until argumentation becomes repetitive.

   h. Call for a vote that will end the debate.

   i. Vote on the legislation.

   j. Adjourn.

7. Ask the students to write justifications for their votes.

Format suggestion *(This may be modified, but is a suggestion for a one-hour session)*

Main motion, opening debate	1 minute
Read bill	1 minute
Affirmative Speaker	1-3 minutes
Questions	2 minutes
Negative Speaker	1-3 minutes
Questions	2 minutes
(Alternate in the same manner until debate becomes repetitive)	
Move to end debate	1 minute
Vote on legislation	2 minutes
Adjourn	1 minute
Write justification for vote	5-6 minutes

Teacher Tips

1. You will need at least three bills to allow all students to speak without too much repetition.

2. Allow students to do some evaluation of their peers.

3. Evaluate and grade the speaker's best speech

Evaluation

1. Collect notes and written justifications and share with students.

2. Fill out the Classroom Congress Critique for each participant.

Bills and Resolutions

The following examples highlight the differences in style and format between a bill and a resolution and show how a variety of solutions might be offered when dealing with a particular current issue. A bill or resolution **must** call for a change in current policy.

A Resolution presents a philosophical statement with three or four reasons for the stand. A resolution does not require a specific course of action.

Example of a Resolution
Desecration of the American Flag

1   **Whereas**, the American flag is the most noticeable symbol of
2   the United States, and
3   **Whereas**, thousands of Americans have died in defense of that
4   symbol, and
5   **Whereas**, the burning of the American flag has historically
6   represented a disrespect for American ideals and policies;
7   **Therefore,** be it resolved by this assembly that a constitutional
8   amendment should be passed making desecration of the American
9   flag illegal.

A Bill creates a specific plan to solve a problem. A bill requires identification of an agency to carry out the plan, funding provisions, timelines for enactment, and enforcement procedures.

Example of a Bill
Classroom Cheating

1   Be it enacted by this assembly that:
2   **Section 1.** Every student caught cheating on standardized tests,
3   classroom tests or assignments will have a permanent disciplinary
4   notice attached to the student transcript.
5   **Section 2.** Every time a student is required to provide a
6   transcript for college application, scholarship application or job
7   application, the "notice of cheating" is to be forwarded as well.
8   **Section 3.** Said student is permanently suspended from all
9   extracurricular activities for the duration of his/her high school
10   career.

Congress Conventions

Beginning Discussion

Chair: The Chair is open to new business.

Member A: [Mister/Madam] Chairman.

Chair: The Chair recognizes [identifies Member A].

Member A: I move that the first period at Stagg begin at 8:00 a.m.

Chair: Is there a second?

Member B: I second it.

Chair: It has been moved and seconded that the first period at Stagg begin at 8:00 a.m. Is there any discussion?

Conducting Discussion

Each member who wishes to speak for or against the motion may stand and be recognized to speak.

At the End of Discussion

Voice Vote

Chair: All those in favor of the motion that the first period at Stagg begin at 8:00 a.m. signify by saying aye; (pause) all those opposed say nay.

Counted Vote

Chair: All those in favor of the motion that the first period at Stagg begin at 8:00 a.m. signify by raising your hand. (count the votes) All opposed raise your hand. (count the votes)

Roll Call Vote

Chair: All those in favor of the motion that the first period at Stagg begin at 8:00 a.m. signify by responding aye and all of those opposed signify by responding nay to a roll call. The secretary will call the roll. (If there is no secretary the Chair should call the roll.)

After the Vote Has Been Completed

Chair: The ayes have it and the motion is carried.

        or

    The nays have it and the motion is defeated.

Chair: The Chair is not open for further business.

Classroom Congress Critique

Presiding Officer_____Session_____

	Shall We Call You Senator?	Impres-sive!	Good	So-So	What Were You Thinking?	Comments
Maintained control	5	4	3	2	1	
Time equity	5	4	3	2	1	
Time accuracy	5	4	3	2	1	
Parliamentary Procedure	5	4	3	2	1	

Speaker_____Bill_____

	Shall We Call You Senator?	Impres-sive!	Good	So-So	What Were You Thinking?	Comments
Intro/Conclusion	5	4	3	2	1	
CLASH w/ opposition	5	4	3	2	1	
Time accuracy	5	4	3	2	1	
Evidence	5	4	3	2	1	

SECTION II
Group Discussion

Classroom discussion often disintegrates due to lack of structure and equity. The following group activities are designed to sustain an organized and fair discussion while working toward goals of cooperation and mutual understanding.

The Literary Fishbowl

An organized, focused discussion on a literary work.

Materials
Sample Invitation
Scoring Criteria for Group Presentations
Fishbowl Evaluation Form

Procedure
1. Several days before the discussion, distribute an invitation to students who will participate in the fishbowl.
2. Instruct students to write three to five starter questions prior to the discussion. The questions should be:
   a. Based on a passage from a text being studied in class
   b. Of interest to them
   c. Have no right or wrong answer
      For example:
      • On page 147 of *Picture Bride*, Mary's husband reveals that he loves Mary because "She knew nothing, was eager to learn and ready to do anything to please him." Do you think that their marriage will endure?
      • The March 31 issue of *Newsweek* reported that President Bush's press secretary said "Democracy will come to Iraq." Do you think this is likely?
3. Explain to the students that they will observe a group of six to ten students discussing an issue based on a text the class is reading. Distribute and review the Scoring Criteria for Group Presentations.
4. Have the class prepare for the discussion by reading and making notes on the text.
5. Schedule the discussions, allowing 30–45 minutes for each.
6. At the beginning of the discussion, each participant shares one question about the story. All participants pose a question before any are answered.
7. Collaboratively, decide on one of the questions to begin the discussion.
8. Allow the discussion to develop naturally from the initial question. Return to other questions as needed; pose and respond to new ones that arise.
9. Continue the discussion for the time allotted, exploring the topic or issue as fully as possible.
10. After you have assessed the students, return the evaluation form to the participants and ask them to complete the self-evaluation portion of the form.

Teacher Tips
1. You can have students write a reflection about how they might improve their own contributions in future discussions.
2. You can have the spectator students be responsible for evaluating the fishbowl participants.

Evaluation
1. Those invited into the fishbowl can receive points for:
   • Their notes/questions
   • Contribution to the discussion
   • Class members' evaluations of them (Fishbowl Evaluation Form)

- Teacher's evaluations based on Scoring Criteria for Group Presentations
- A written reflection on what they learned about the topic or issue during the discussion and how they fulfilled their role

2. Those observing the fishbowl will receive points for:
   - Their notes/questions
   - A written reflection on what they learned about the topic during the discussion and any comments or questions that remain unanswered
   - Their evaluation of assigned participants (optional)

Sample Invitation

Dear _____ ,

You have been chosen to participate in our next fishbowl discussion.

This will take place on _____ ,

and will cover _____ .

Please prepare your questions and notes thoroughly.

We are looking forward to having your insights.

Appreciatively,

Scoring Criteria for Group Presentations

	Scoring Criteria	Exceptional 5	Accomplished 4	Competent 3	Developing 2 / 1
Group	**Organization** Introduction/conclusion Separation of ideas Clear, logical order Transitions Internal summaries	Introduction attention-getting, memorable, appropriate; clear separation of balanced ideas; signposts; parallel structure evident; complete summaries separating ideas; linkages set up progression; clarifies ideas when needed; internal summaries used to enrich discussion.	Introduction attention-getting, clear; ideas are separate, not necessarily balanced/clear; reasonable order in presenting ideas; short separation of ideas; linkages are obvious; summaries used mechanically; clarifies some idea.	Introduction evident; main ideas of topic covered; order evident; transitions are simple in structure; summaries occasionally used.	Unclear/undeveloped introduction/conclusion; incomplete coverage of ideas; some order evident; few transitions; summaries rarely used.
Group	**Research** Factual information Interviews Validity of sources Breadth of sources	Uses information that is relevant, authoritative, clear, timely, precise; sources reflect audience analysis; multiple authorities used; recognized authoritative and specialized sources used; recognizes biases of sources; in depth, thorough research; comprehensive sources; all viewpoints considered.	Often uses information that is relevant, authoritative, clear, timely, precise; multiple sources used; relies on a variety of outside sources; is aware of some resources; variety of sources; viewpoints varied.	Use of information is generalized; more opinions and own beliefs relied upon; some sources used; uses popular, easily obtainable material; cross-section of materials used.	Uses preponderance of opinions and own beliefs; some facts; limited range of sources used; uses biased or unreliable sources; limited viewpoints.
Group	**Cooperation** Balanced participation Courtesy Listening/responding Staying on topic	All members participate equally; expression/acceptance/encouragement of divergent opinions; pronounced display of respect for opinions/positions of others, recognition of others' feelings; active, critical listeners, encourage meaningful feedback of discussants; all remarks precise and relevant.	All members encouraged to participate; expression of a variety of viewpoints; shows respect for positions/opinions of others; has empathy for all members; attentive listeners; give meaningful feedback; remarks pertain to topic.	All members contribute ideas; variety of viewpoints may be expressed; acknowledges rights of others to express viewpoints; polite; respectful; gives some feedback; most remarks relevant.	Unequal contributions by members; information may be one-sided; exhibit some lack of understanding for other's rights; passive listeners, feedback lacking or inappropriate; many remarks digressive.
Individual	**Speaker** Use of facts and ideas Participation/response Delivery Cooperation with group	Comments are supported with empirical data; eager participant; comments reflect in-depth understanding; fluent; audience impetus; verbally and nonverbally commanding; inspires discussion; diplomatic; attempts to elicit opinions from more reticent participants.	Uses outside sources to support comments; enthusiastic participant; comments reflect knowledgeable understanding; smooth, enthusiastic, audience-directed delivery; encourages discussion; senses dynamics of group; tactful.	Some outside information cited to support comments; active participant; comments indicate reasonable understanding; clear, proficient delivery; related to audience; generates discusions; interacts with group.	Limited use of outside data to support statements; occasional participant; comments indicate limited understanding; delivery understandable, adequate; aware of audience; cooperates in discussion; interacts passively with group.

Fishbowl Evaluation Form

Name_____

	Swimmer	Treader	Floater	Comments
Thoughtful and thought-provoking questions	3	2	I	
Insightful contribution to the group	3	2	I	
Introspective reflection on the discussion	3	2	I	

Self-Evaluation for Fishbowl Participants

As you exit the bowl, comment on . . .

1. What insights did you carry out of the bowl? This can be about the process or the text—or both. Be specific!
2. What was your best contribution to the bowl?
3. What questions about the issue or topic do you still have that remain unanswered?

Collaborative Reading Groups

Collaborative Reading Groups allow students to share the task of reading texts, to share insights and to engage in a discussion of the work.

Materials

Sample Collaborative Reading

Procedure

1. Determine the study questions for the text the groups will be reading.
2. Divide the class into groups and assign, or have the group assign, speaking roles.
3. Prepare a worksheet similar to the Sample Collaborative Reading, listing the different parts and the study questions.
4. Prior to the activity, define the terms and concepts the study group will discuss.
5. Outline the rules and procedures for the reading:
   a. Each group will have a recorder who will interrupt the reading on each page that has a question.
   b. The group will work together to decide on the answers, using a dictionary when necessary.
   c. The recorder will write down the agreed on response.
   d. Everyone is responsible for the information on all questions.
   e. Students will be given a quiz on one of the study questions at the end of the day. They won't know which question will be on the quiz.

Teacher Tips

1. If you are working with a play, you will want to combine smaller characters into larger parts.
2. Accommodate group size to the differing number of parts.
3. Ask a student with a small part or role to act as the recorder.
4. Keying the questions to specific scenes in the play or paragraphs in a text will allow students to concentrate on the reading.

Evaluation

1. You can assign participation points for reading each day.
2. Give points for the specific study questions and the final question.
3. Use a selected study question as an end-of-activity quiz.

Sample Collaborative Reading

Œdipus Rex

Roles	Day 1 Readers	Day 2 Readers
Choragos		
Jocasta		
Kreon		
Messengers		
Œdipus		
Priest		
Shepherd		
Teiresias		
CHORUS antistrophe		
CHORUS strophe		

Questions

Page _____, Line _____. According to the priest, what is the specific nature of the plague that visited Thebes? Metaphorically, how does this connect with Œdipus' "crimes"?

Page _____, Line _____. Why is there tragic irony in Œdipus' line "Sick as you are, not one is as sick as I"?

Page _____, Line _____. What is the curse that Œdipus puts upon the murderers of Laios? How is this tragically ironic?

Page _____, Line _____. Œdipus reveals his temper in his tirade with Teiresias. Yet Teiresias persists with his truths. How is Teiresias's list of contradictions actually a list of paradoxes? Prove it!

Page _____, Line _____. Jocasta sets Œdipus's mind at rest by offering proof that oracles sometimes make mistakes. Why is there irony in her proof?

Page _____, Line _____. "Oh riddlers of God's will, where are you now?" What is hubris and why is Jocasta guilty of it to the tenth degree?

Page _____, Line _____. Why is Œdipus's predicament of whether or not to believe the prophecies a true dilemma?

Page _____, Line _____. Based on Jocasta's commentary about dreams and desires, what in Freudian analysis is an Œdipal Complex? (Use your dictionary if you're still confused.)

Page _____, Line _____. Œdipus chooses blindness rather than suicide. Speculate as to why this is more dramatically appropriate—given what he's done and said.

Page _____, Line _____. Œdipus tells his children that he had neither sight nor knowledge before. What is Sophocles suggesting about knowledge?

At the end of the play, consider Aristotle's definition of tragedy. Do you feel purged of pity and fear as you read the final lines of the play? Explain.

Philosophical Chairs

A technique to allow students to critically think, verbally ponder, and logically write their beliefs.

Materials

Question Levels and Sample Questions that Lead to Philosophical Statements
Philosophical Chairs Seating Arrangement
Philosophical Chairs Rules of Engagement
Philosophical Chairs Written Evaluation Sheet
Philosophical Chairs Score Sheet

Procedure

1. Ask the students to read a newspaper article, short story, essay or literary selection, prior to coming to class. Tell them to take notes as they read and bring these notes to class.
2. After the students have finished reading and taking notes, present them with a second or third level question that will elicit a philosophical statement. (See Question Levels and Sample Questions that Lead to Philosophical Statements.) You can provide a philosophical statement for the first few discussions and allow students to collaborate on future philosophical statements if so desired.
3. Place the chairs in a horseshoe seating arrangement, with the two ends longer than the back (see Philosophical Chairs Seating Arrangement).
4. Tell the students that they will argue the merits of the philosophical statement and that their choice of seat during the discussion will illustrate their position. If they agree with the statement, they should sit on the right; if they disagree with the statement, they should sit on the left. If they are "undecided," they should sit at the back of the horseshoe. They will have the opportunity to move as their minds change. At the end of the discussion, they must determine which position to adopt.
5. Choose a student moderator whose job is to see that everyone gets a chance to speak.
6. Hand out and review copies of Philosophical Chairs Rules of Engagement or your own rules.
7. Set a time limit for the discussion, and tell the students that they must speak at least two times to gain full credit.
8. The moderator can present the first question and invite a participant to the hot seat to speak.
9. Following the first speaker, another speaker may volunteer to sit in the hot seat and speak. If necessary, the moderator can maintain a priority list of those students who have raised their hands to speak.

Teacher Tips

1. Set ground rules about the discussion before it starts.
2. Require students to summarize the previous speaker before they present their arguments.
3. You should moderate the first and, if needed, the second discussion.
4. If class is too large to involve all the students at the same time, you can have a subsection discuss the statement. Have that group take notes and then debrief the rest of the class as to who had the "pivotal point(s)" that ultimately persuaded adoption of one side or the other.

Evaluation

1. Have the students write a personal reflection, responding to questions related to the material read.
2. Have them assess the activity using the Philosophical Chairs Written Evaluation Sheet.
3. Use the Philosophical Chairs Score Sheet to assess student speeches.

Question Levels and Sample Questions
that Lead to Philosophical Statements

Question Levels

Level One Questions Will:

Define

Describe

Identify

List

Name

Observe

Recite

Do not use the above in forming questions for "Philosophical Chairs." The debate will not flow nor will there be the conflict needed to have a successful experience.

Level Two Questions Will:

Analyze

Compare

Contrast

Group

Determine

Infer

Sequence

Synthesize

Level Three Questions Will:

Apply a principle

Evaluate

Hypothesize

Imagine

Judge

Predict

Speculate

Use the above in forming questions that generate statements for discussion. They allow for more ideas and different beliefs to be expressed more freely, which is what the debate wants.

Sample Opening Philosophical Statements

While reading *Hamlet* by William Shakespeare:

In Act V scene 2, Fortinbras Says:

> "Let four captains
> Bear Hamlet like a soldier to the stage,
> For he was likely, had he been put on,
> To have proved most royal; and for his passage,
> The soldier's music and the rite of war
> Speak loudly for him."

Fortinbras feels that Hamlet would have made a good soldier. What he does not know is that Hamlet was at war with his uncle and had acted as a soldier. Evaluate this statement by agreeing or disagreeing with it.

While reading "Civil Disobedience" by Henry David Thoreau:

> "The government is best which governs least."

If acts of civil disobedience do not harm the government or its people, analyze whether jailing those who commit those acts is useless.

While reading *To Kill a Mockingbird* by Harper Lee:

In chapters 1 through 6, we meet Jem, Scout, Atticus and Dill, as well as other members of Maycomb community. The children, Scout, Jem and especially Dill, are obsessed with the Finch's neighbor Boo Radley. The obsession creates problems for both Boo Radley and the Finches. Compare whether the need to know is more important than personal privacy.

More Topics for Philosophical Discussion

1. Hypothesize whether most people care enough about the environment to make personal sacrifices to save it.
2. Infer the validity of the United States selling arms to any foreign country.
3. Judge whether students should be able to select their own teachers.
4. Determine whether children should ever be physically punished.
5. Evaluate whether unclaimed animals in the pound should be used for medical research.
6. Judge whether it was easier to grow up when my parents were kids than it is for me now.
7. Speculate whether legalization of drugs would result in less crime.
8. Determine whether any censorship of music or art is wrong.
9. Evaluate whether rock music contributes to a rebellious attitude in some teenagers.
10. Apply the principle that every student has the opportunity to succeed in our school.

Philosophical Chairs Seating Arrangement

" Y E S — A G R E E "

Hot Seat

"U N D E C I D E D"

" N O — D I S A G R E E "

Philosophical Chairs Rules of Engagement

1. Read the material for the debate and the opening statement carefully; be sure you understand it.

2. Listen to the person who is speaking.

3. Acknowledge another person's point of view (e.g., " Max stated _____; however, I believe that_____.").

4. Contribute your own thoughts, offering your reasons as succinctly as possible.

5. Respond to statements only, not to the personality of the person giving them.

6. Be open to changing your mind about the statement as new information or reasoning is presented.

7. Move to the opposite side or to the undecided chairs as your thinking grows and changes.

8. Support the moderator in maintaining order and helping the discussion to progress.

9. Reflect on the experience via the closing activity or assignment.

Philosophical Chairs Written Evaluation Sheet

Please respond candidly and specifically to the following questions:

1. What was the most frustrating portion of the exercise?

2. What was the most successful portion of the exercise?

3. What was said that caused you to change your seat, or what was said that caused you not to change your seat?

4. What conclusions can you draw about how you form your beliefs?

5. What conclusion can you draw about the nature of forming beliefs as it might relate to this activity?

Philosophical Chairs Score Sheet

Name _____ Evaluator _____
Topic _____ Date _____

Speech One

	Outstanding Use	Excellent Use	Acceptable Use	Little Use	Not Used	Comments
Summary of Previous Speech	5	4	3	2	1	
Thoughtful Reflection	5	4	3	2	1	
Use of Specific Examples	5	4	3	2	1	
Usage and Grammar	5	4	3	2	1	
Total						

Speech Two

	Outstanding Use	Excellent Use	Acceptable Use	Little Use	Not Used	Comments
Summary of Previous Speech	5	4	3	2	1	
Thoughtful Reflection	5	4	3	2	1	
Use of Specific Examples	5	4	3	2	1	
Usage and Grammar	5	4	3	2	1	
Total						

SECTION III
Informative and Persuasive Speaking

Students frequently must write reports of information or persuasion in a variety of subject areas. This section will enhance the skills needed to present this information effectively. Students develop outlining, research, writing, argumentation, and speaking skills they can utilize in a variety of situations.

Scrambled Outline of a Speech

An exercise familiarizing students with the elements of outlining
and organizing in preparation for eventually writing an outline.

Materials

Sample Outline for an Informative Speech

Organization Strategies

Scrambled Outline of a Speech Assignment Sheet

Procedure

1. Review the elements of an outline using Sample Outline for an Informative Speech or an outline of your choice.
2. Distribute Organization Strategies and review planning the body of an outline.
3. Hand out the Scrambled Outline of a Speech Assignment Sheet and review with the class.

Evaluation

Assess the final outlines on form only—save content assessment for later outlines on topics of their choice.

Sample Outline for an Informative Speech

Content: Serial Killers
Intent: to tell about the characteristics of serial killers

I. **Introduction:** Theodore Robert Bundy was a handsome and intelligent man whose brains and irresistible charm gave him a promising start in life. At 25, he had earned a degree in psychology, had served as campaign aide to Washington's governor, had written about rape prevention for the Seattle Crime Commission, and four years later had started law school in Utah. This would have been the perfect success story if it weren't for one thing: Ted Bundy was a serial murderer. Known as the "killer with a thousand faces," Ted Bundy was a gallery of presentable identities, but only his victims saw the true face of the man who may have murdered 40 women and girls in four years.

II. **Thesis:** Serial killers have clear characteristics and patterns.

III. **Body:**

    A. Description of situation in America

        1. Rates in U.S. alone (Evidence Card #1, *Newsweek*, 1985)

        2. Statistics in U.S. compared to others (VISUAL: graph)

          a) World population *vs.* number of murderers

          b) U.S. population *vs.* number of murderers (Evidence Card #2, Cook, 1985)

    B. Description of criminals

        1. Family characteristics

          a) Parents troubled

            (1) Mothers unwed

            (2) Fathers violent or abusive

          b) Children abused

        2. Personal characteristics (Evidence Card #3, Miller, 1983)

          a) Behavioral characteristics

            (1) Bedwetting

            (2) Hallucinations

          b) Physiological characteristics (VISUAL: drawing)

    C. Description of pattern (VISUAL: poster)

Conclusion: The serial murderer may follow his pattern for decades until he is sick to death of his own disease and purposely gets caught. But until he does this, there is little hope of stopping him. The characteristics and patterns of serial killers are clean, but as for catching them, chasing serial killers is like chasing bolts of lightning: they strike without warning and are gone.

Organization Strategies

The type of plan you use will be determined by the kind of information you wish to convey.

The Time Plan: Describes a sequence of events in order.
1. BODY (time):
   A. What happened first
   B. What happened second
   C. What happened third

Use this plan to tell a story, trace historical events, or describe a process.

The Space Plan: Describes arrangements of parts and/or their relationships.
1. BODY (space):
   A. One location
   B. Another location
   C. And another location

Use this plan to explain a place, a structure.

The Topical Plan: Explains significant topics of categories within a content area.
1. BODY (topical):
   A. Topic 1
   B. Topic 2
   C. Topic 3

Use this plan to explain selected categories or topics such as advantages/disadvantages, reasons, important aspects, skills or characteristics.

The Cause-Effect Plan: Explains the situation and its cause and/or effects.
1. BODY (cause-effect):
   A. Description of situation
   B. Explanation of causes
   C. Explanation of effects

Use this plan to explain the description of a situation (like homelessness) and its causes (unemployment, reduced medical care, bad choices) or its effects (increased welfare costs, increased crime, increased violence).

Scrambled Outline of a Speech Assignment Sheet

Due Date _____

Scrambled Lists

Directions: Below are four sets of information in completely random order. Your task is to write the content, intent, and organizational plan for each set and then arrange the items in proper outline form. The content is included in the list. You will have to create the intent statement. You do not have to write out the introduction, thesis, and conclusion, but you do need to include the Roman numeral, the label, and space for these items to be written. ***Do the work for each outline on a separate sheet of paper.***

Content (This is in the list.):

Intent (You will create this after you discover the point of the speech.):

I. **Introduction:** (Don't write this yet. Just put the labels and leave two lines of space for it.)

II. **Thesis:** (Don't write this yet, either. Just put the labels and leave two lines of space for it.)

III. **Body:** (Plan: Label the type of plan after you review the set of words.)
   For the **body** of each set arrange the words properly.
   - Ideas that are labeled the same must coordinate; that is, they must have the same level of generality (e.g., dirty water and clean water; not water containing industrial pollutants and clean water).
   - Ideas that are labeled the same must be parallel; that is, they must be worded the same way (e.g., water pollution in our community and water pollution in our nation; not water pollution in our community and national concerns about toxic water).
   - If you have a "1" in your outline, you must have a "2" in your outline; if you have an "A," you must have a "B."
   - All the terms in each list must be used as they are. You must not change terms.

IV. **Conclusion:** Don't write this yet. Just put the number and label and leave space for it.

Set One

Unclean swimming water
Filtration plants
Water pollution
Conservation efforts
Difficulties caused by water pollution
Undesirable fishing water
Sewage disposal laws
Unsafe drinking water
Cures for water pollution

Set Two

Redwoods (CA)
Disneyland
Oregon
Grand Coulee Dam (WA)
Mount Hood (OR)
Chinatown
Washington
Yosemite
Seattle (WA)
Portland (OR)
California
Puget Sound (WA)
Tour of the West Coast
Fisherman's Wharf
Oregon Caves (OR)
San Francisco

Set Three

Fog
Lines
Hatches closed
Foul weather gear
Tools
Gather gear
Main sail
Sails
Preparation for sailing
Gear stowed
Check weather bureau
Winds
Rig the boat
Rain
Tides
Change of clothes
Food
Lines secured
Jib sail
Sails set
Personal gear

Set Four

Bonfires
Damage to personal health
Results of smog
Smog
Factories
Lungs polluted
Origins of smog
Watering eyes
Automobiles
Burning eyes
Irritated eyes

A Speech to Inform: All About Me

An opportunity for students to introduce themselves to any course.

Materials

Scoring Criteria for Original Oral Presentations
All About Me Assignment Sheet
Using Visual Aids
Appendix 8: Writing an Introduction
Appendix 9: Writing a Conclusion
Appendix 7: Warm Up Exercises (optional)

Procedure

1. Review the elements of an original speech and good speaking skills by handing out Scoring Criteria for Original Oral Presentations.
2. Distribute the All About Me Assignment Sheet and review.
3. Ask the students to interview at least two family members, friends, or teachers and ask them what they think of the student and why. What do they think makes him/her "tick"? Tell students to use quotes to support their information.
4. Let them be creative: Students may use visual aids such as pictures, posters, the family crest, etc. Distribute and discuss Using Visual Aids.
5. Instruct students to follow the outline format in developing their presentations. If necessary review outlining procedure, facilitating Scrambled Outline of a Speech on page 68.
6. Review the rules that will govern the presentations and the criteria for assessment.
7. Remind students that when preparing their speeches they should:
   • use an attention-getter introduction (see Appendix 8)
   • make sure they have a strong conclusion (see Appendix 9)
   • work hard on body control
   • incorporate gestures.

Teacher Tips

1. This activity is an excellent starter for seniors preparing to write their college application essays.
2. You may have to limit the types of visual aids used depending on the audiovisual equipment available.
3. If the speakers need invigorating, employ the warm up exercises from Appendix 7.

Evaluation

1. Evaluate students based on the Scoring Criteria for Original Oral Presentations.
2. You can limit the number of criteria assessed if this is the students' first oral presentation of the year.

Scoring Criteria for Original Oral Presentation

Scoring Criteria	Exceptional 5	Accomplished 4	Competent 3	Developing 2 / 1
Structural/ Organizational Conventions Introduction Main Ideas Supporting materials Conclusion	• Clever attention getter; clear, imaginative thesis and preview. • Main Ideas equal and separate with ample support material. • Connected by original transitions, logical throughout; creative pattern. • Conclusion ties speech together—leaves audience with memorable message.	• Attention-getter, clear thesis and preview. • Main ideas support thesis. • Support material is appropriate. • Organizational pattern is clear, transitions are clear and appropriate. • Conclusion summarizes, ties to introduction and leaves audience with a final thought.	• Introduction used, but may not lead smoothly to thesis. • Thesis is clear, but may be worded incorrectly. • Main points may not be worded clearly, but organization is apparent. • Uses a conclusion that summarizes.	• States topic as introduction or begins with thesis. • Not clear organizational pattern, rambling comments lack structure. • Expresses many unsupported opinions. Conclusion brief, undeveloped: "Well, that's it."
Appropriate- ness of content/ language For audience For purpose For assignment	• Speaker has obviously considered the audience. • Examples and words are creative and well-chosen. • Speaker displays a clear understanding of assignment and purpose.	• Speaker makes limited use of knowledge of audience. • Speaker meets requirements of assignment.	• Speaker makes token acknowledgment of audience. • Basic compliance with requirements of assignment.	• No adjustment to audience. • Strays from assignment. • Makes inappropriate comments, uses slang or inappropriate language.
Physical Expression Eye contact Posture Gesture Movement	• Strong eye contact with entire audience. • Posture is strong, commanding and purposeful. • May forego podium. • Gestures and movement are natural and effective.	• Sustains eye contact with audience, stands with purpose. • Uses some gestures and movement to enhance message.	• Eye contact is sporadic; speaker may look at only one part of audience or may use notes frequently. • Uses podium. • Uses few gestures and limited or no movement.	• Avoids eye contact; may read from notes or rarely glance at audience. • May slouch or lean on podium. • May be stiff. • Gestures/movement are inappropriate, nervous, stiff, or nonexistent.

Scoring Criteria for Original Oral Presentation, continued.

Scoring Criteria	Exceptional 5	Accomplished 4	Competent 3	Developing 2 / 1
Vocal Expression Rate too fast/slow Volume too loud/soft Pitch too high/low Articulation/pronunciation	• Speaker is enjoyable to hear; uses expression and emphasis. • Tone is conversational, but with purpose. • Voice sounds natural, neither patterned nor monotone. • Speaker pronounces words clearly and correctly.	• Speaker speaks clearly, using expression. Conversational style is evident, but spontaneity may be lacking. Speaker's pace and volume make speech easy to listen to and understand.	• Speaker may lack spontaneity and/or conversational style. • A vocal pattern or monotone may be apparent. Volume may be too soft or rate too fast.	• Speaker makes little attempt to use vocal techniques to communicate. • Displays a variety of weaknesses: monotone, soft volume, hesitation, verbal "fillers" (uh, um, y'know), giggling.
Overall Impact Energy Enthusiasm Sincerity Originality/creativity	• Speaker appears to believe strongly in message and demonstrates desire to have the audience listen, understand, and remember. • Overall presentation is creative and exciting.	• Speaker appears to believe in message and is well-prepared, displaying confident control of information. • Speaker makes clear attempt to communicate with audience.	• Speaker displays good preparation, but may lack confidence and enthusiasm. • Speaker speaks more to fulfill assignment than to communicate with audience.	• Speaker creates impression of being inadequately prepared. • Speaker lacks confidence and enthusiasm. • Little attempt to communicate effectively with audience.
Optional Features Audio Visual Multimedia	• Speaker uses a variety of objects, charts, graphs, etc., effectively to support and clarify the message. • Materials used are quality products, easy to see, hear.	• Speaker uses some objects, charts, graphs, etc., effectively to support and clarify the message. • Materials used are quality products, easy to see, hear.	• Speaker uses some objects, charts, graphs, etc; sometimes use does not enhance message; quality may be inconsistent.	• Speaker uses insufficient aids or misuses aids; aids of poor quality.

All About Me Assignment Sheet

This is a speech about you! It is not just what you know about you, but rather what others think about you as well.

Preparing Your Speech
Your speech must include:
- Birth information: Birthday, place of birth
- Places you have lived
- Family members: Including parents' names, brothers, and sisters
- Your family tree: Is there an ancestor who did something significant or special that you'd like to share?
- Favorites: Food, colors, clothing, pets, hobbies, interests, books, music, art. What general things are of interest to you and why?
- Travels: Any special trips, close or far away, which you would recommend.
- What makes you tick. This is the major part of your speech. Interview at least two family members, friends, or teachers and ask them what they think of you and why.

You might want to consider these questions:
1. What is my strongest asset?
2. Why is the world a better place because I'm in it?
3. What is your most vivid memory of my childhood?
4. What is the nicest thing I have ever done for you?
5. What do you see me doing in 10 years?
6. Can you suggest an item that would signify what type of person I am?
7. What motivates me?

Use the outline format to organize your speech.

Be creative! You may use visual aids such as pictures and posters, but do not use video tapes or slides.

Remember to use an attention-getter introduction and a strong conclusion. Start strong and stay strong!

Work on body control and try to incorporate gestures.

Presenting Your Speech
1. The introduction and conclusion should be the only memorized parts of your speech.
2. You should deliver your speech in an extemporaneous manner using speaking notes.
3. You may use one (1) note card, no larger than 3 x 5, but you may use both sides of the card. You may not "micro-write" your speech onto card because you should be speaking from your outline.
4. Speeches must be 4–6 minutes long. Those shorter or longer will be penalized.

Using Visual Aids

A great deal of our conversation takes place in sight of the objects about which we are speaking. Seeing an actual object can clarify meaning for the audience. Television, for example, has an advantage over radio in conveying a message not only because speakers can be seen as well as heard, but also because it can use visual aids to supplement the spoken word. Visual and auditory aids include charts, maps, graphs, diagrams, pictures, posters, models, tapes, and objects. (For purposes of this class, slides and video tapes are not permitted.) These aids are particularly useful in teaching and other types of informative speaking.

Tips for Using Visual Aids:

- Use visual aids only when they will help the audience better understand what you are saying. If your topic is abstract, you may have to be extremely creative to develop ideas for visual aids.
- Do not overdo the use of visual aids.
- You must explain your ideas in words and use the visual aids to make the ideas clearer. Visual aids do not substitute for explanation.
- Be certain your visual aids are easy for the entire audience to see and comprehend. Make drawings simple. Use vivid colors. Note: *Red and yellow are difficult to see!*
- Talk to the audience, not to the visual aid.
- Make sure visual aids are in order and audio and/or visual tapes are cued up, before you speak.

You must use your visual aids as you speak. Synchronize the use of the aids with your speaking; that is, show visual aids only when you are talking about them and talk about the visual aid only while you are showing it.

A Speech to Inform: Picture Speech

An opportunity for students to introduce themselves in any course.

Materials

Scoring Criteria for Original Oral Presentations (page 71–72).

Picture Speech Assignment Sheet

Peer Review of an Informative Speech

Informative Speech Scoring Guide

Peer Critique for the Informative Speech

Appendix 8: Writing an Introduction

Appendix 9: Writing a Conclusion

Appendix 7: Warm Up Exercises (optional)

Procedure

1. Review the elements of an original speech and good speaking skills by handing out Scoring Criteria for Original Oral Presentations.
2. Tell students they will be developing introductory speeches based on types of pictures. Distribute the Picture Speech Assignment Sheet and review.
3. Instruct students to follow the outline format in developing their presentations. If necessary review outlining procedure, facilitating Scrambled Outline of a Speech on page 68.
4. Review the rules that will govern the presentations.
5. Remind students that when preparing their speeches they should:
   - use an attention-getter introduction (see Appendix 8)
   - make sure they have a strong conclusion (see Appendix 9)
   - work hard on body control
   - incorporate gestures.
6. Using Peer Review of an Informative Speech, students can review each other's presentations in small groups prior to presenting to the entire class.
7. If the speakers need invigorating, employ the warm up exercises from Appendix 7.

Evaluation

1. Use the Informative Speech Scoring Guide to evaluate the speeches.
2. Students can evaluate each other using the Peer Critique for the Informative Speech.

Note: All of the evaluative tools are based on the elements of the Scoring Criteria for Original Oral Presentations.

Picture Speech Assignment Sheet

Develop your speech around one of the following types of pictures. Remember that you will have to bring the picture to your presentation, so it must be large enough for the class to see clearly.

Animal: Choose an animal that most represents you or an animal whose traits you most admire.

> *Example:* The lioness and I are aggressive, loving, and loyal.
>
> *Example:* I would like to have the qualities of a gazelle because they are athletic, attractive, and social.

Person: Choose a person you admire or with whom you would want to change places.

> *Example:* I admire Gandhi because he was courageous, peaceful and loving.
>
> *Example:* I want to be more like Wayne Gretzky because he is articulate, intelligent and athletic.

Place: Choose a place that reflects your personality or one where you would like to live.

> *Example:* This picture of the shore represents my moods of calmness, turmoil, and tranquillity.
>
> *Example:* I love Hawaii because of the weather, scenery and people.

Objects: Choose an object with a function that illustrates the qualities you would like to emulate.

> *Example:* This computer is accurate, valuable, and essential—all qualities I'm working to foster in my own personality.

Use the outline format to organize your speech.

Remember to use an attention-getter introduction and a strong conclusion. Start strong and stay strong!

Work on body control and try to incorporate gestures.

Presenting Your Speech

1. The introduction and conclusion should be the only memorized parts of your speech.
2. You should deliver your speech in an extemporaneous manner using speaking notes.
3. You may use one (1) note card, no larger than 3 x 5, but you may use both sides of the card. You may not "micro-write" your speech onto card because you should be speaking from your outline.
4. Speeches must be 2–4 minutes long. Those shorter or longer will be penalized.
5. Remember to bring your picture!

Peer Review of an Informative Speech

Name of Speaker _____

Please indicate: 1=got it!   2=almost   3=say what?

_____ eye contact   _____ preparation

_____ rate of speaking   _____ enthusiasm/energy

_____ volume   _____ eye-contact

_____ acceptable grammar   _____ gestures

_____ posture and poise   _____ interaction with visuals

I especially liked

To improve your speech I suggest that you

Informative Speech Scoring Guide

Scoring Criteria	Exceptional	Accomplished	Competent	Developing	Comments
Organization Introduction Conclusion Main Ideas Supporting Info	5	4	3	2 / 1	
Audience Appeal Language Content Clear Purpose	5	4	3	2 / 1	
Delivery Eye contact Gesture Vocal Expression Posture Time: _____	5	4	3	2 / 1	
Overall Preparation Energy Creativity	5	4	3	2 / 1	

Comments:

Recommendations:

Peer Critique for the Informative Speech

Speaker_____ Time _____

Topic:_____

"Wow! I didn't know that before!"
Here are some things that I learned from your speech:

"Bravo!"
Overall, I was most impressed by these elements of your . . .

    Structure

    Vocal Expression

    Physical Expression

    Overall Impact

If I could give you only one suggestion for improvement it would be:

Critic's Signature_____

A Speech to Inform: I'm the Expert!

An opportunity for students to provide expert information on a topic of your or their choosing.

Materials

Scoring Criteria for Original Oral Presentations (page 71–72)
I'm the Expert Assignment Sheet
I'm the Expert Sample Outline
Using Visual Aids (page 74)
Informative Speech Scoring Guide (page 78)
Peer Critique for the Informative Speech (page 79)
Appendix 8: Writing an Introduction
Appendix 9: Writing a Conclusion
Appendix 7: Warm Up Exercises (optional)

Procedure

1. Review the elements of an original speech and good speaking skills by handing out the Scoring Criteria for Original Oral Presentations.
2. Tell students they will be giving a speech on a topic about which they think they are expert. Distribute I'm the Expert Assignment Sheet and review.
3. Ask the students to follow the outline format in developing their presentations. Hand out I'm the Expert Sample Outline and review. If necessary, facilitate Scrambled Outline of a Speech on page 68.
4. Remind students that they should be creative. They may use visual aids such as pictures and posters. Distribute and discuss Using Visual Aids.
5. Review the rules that will govern the presentations and the criteria for assessment.
6. Remind students that when preparing their speeches they should:
   • use an attention-getter introduction (see Appendix 8)
   • make sure they have a strong conclusion (see Appendix 9)
   • work hard on body control
   • incorporate gestures.

Teacher Tips

1. You may have to limit the types of visuals used depending on the audiovisual equipment available.
2. If the speakers need invigorating, employ the warm up exercises from Appendix 7.

Evaluation

1. Use the Informative Speech Scoring Guide to evaluate the speeches.
2. Students can evaluate each other using Peer Critique for the Informative Speech.

Note: All of the evaluative tools are based on the elements of Scoring Criteria for Original Oral Presentations.

I'm the Expert Assignment Sheet

Preparing Your Speech

1. Choose a topic about which you think you are expert:

   Do choose a topic that:
   - you are interested in (e.g., ballroom dancing)
   - you can discuss in detail without research (e.g., if you have volunteered at a homeless shelter, you could discuss that)

   Do not choose a topic that:
   - would be better demonstrated than explained, i.e., do not tell "how to . . ."
   - is a "list;" i.e., do not tell "what we need to water-ski" or "the rules of . . ."
   - is a recommendation, i.e., the best place(s) to camp/hike/ski/fish/bike ride/hide.
   - is an incident or event, i.e., my experience with a ghost.
   - is expository, i.e., what it takes to be a good diver/gymnast/ student/ friend.

   Do *not* research your topic.

2. Use the outline format to organize your speech.

3. Be creative! You may use visual aids such as picture, posters, but do not use video tapes or slides.

4. Remember to use an attention-getter introduction and a strong conclusion. Start strong and stay strong!

5. Work on body control and try to incorporate gestures.

Presenting Your Speech

1. The introduction and conclusion should be the only memorized parts of your speech.

2. You should deliver your speech in an extemporaneous manner using speaking notes.

3. You may use one (1) note card, no larger than 3 x 5, but may use both sides of the card. You may not "micro-write" speech onto card because you should be speaking from your outline.

4. Speeches must be 4–6 minutes long. Those shorter or longer will be penalized.

I'm the Expert Sample Outline

Content: Deep-sea fishing

Intent: To tell about the events of my deep-sea fishing trip this summer

I. **Introduction:** What does rock 'n' roll mean to you? It meant music to me until this summer when rock became rockfish and roll became the movement of a fishing boat launched from Santa Cruz Yacht Harbor.

II. **Thesis:** My deep-sea fishing trip this summer was an exciting and rewarding experience.

III. **Body (time)**
    A. Preparing for the trip
        1. Making reservations
        2. Filling prescriptions
        3. Fixing refreshments
    B. Taking the trip
        1. Renting gear
        2. Getting settled
          a) The boat
          b) The people
            (1) The workers
            (2) The tourists
        3. Catching fish
          a) Cod
          b) Sandab
          c) Shark
    C. Returning home
        1. Getting fish cleaned
          a) The worker
          b) The watchers
        2. Preparing the fish
          a) BBQ
          b) Bake
          c) Fry

IV. **Conclusion:** While rock 'n' roll music may never be replaced by deep-sea fishing, one thing is certain. The experience of deep-sea fishing is, like rock 'n' roll, a one-of-a-kind adventure.

Demonstration Speech

An exercise on constructing a "how to" speech.

Materials

Demonstration Speech Assignment Sheet

Sample Demonstration Outline (Basic)

Sample Demonstration Outline (Advanced)

Using Visual Aids (page 74)

Demonstration Speech Scoring Guide

Appendix 8: Writing an Introduction

Appendix 9: Writing a Conclusion

Appendix 7: Warm Up Exercises (optional)

Procedure

1. Review the basic elements of a demonstration speech.
2. Tell students to choose a subject/topic they know how to do. Some topics do not work well for demonstrations. Remember that they have to be able to *show* their subject *in the classroom*. Have them consider some of these ideas:

set the table for dinner	origami
dress a wound	transplant a plant
work with clay	make a kite
dance	wrap and decorate a present
wrestling holds	magic
juggling	work a yo yo

3. Review outlining using the sample outlines below. You may want to facilitate Scrambled Outline of a Speech on page 68.
4. Distribute the Demonstration Speech Assignment Sheet and Using Visual Aids and review with the class.
5. Ask students to create a written outline of their speech. Remind them that the outline must be typed or written in blue or black ink in the proper form and must be submitted prior to their speech.
6. Evaluate the outlines and return them to the students for revision if necessary.
7. Hand out the Demonstration Speech Scoring Guide and review thoroughly the criteria for evaluation.

8. Remind students to memorize their introductions and conclusions (see Appendixes 8 and 9).
9. Recommend that they transfer their outlines to 3 x 5 cards so that they can refer to them as they speak.
10. Schedule the presentations.
11. If the speakers need invigorating, employ the warm up exercises from Appendix 7 before the speeches begin.

Teacher Tips
1. Encourage students to search for a tangible object to demonstrate. It should be something that they know quite a bit about and that they are sure will be interesting to the rest of the class. Encourage students to be creative!
2. Make sure that the topics chosen are appropriate for the classroom.
3. If students demonstrate food preparation, tell them to have a "finished product."
4. Remind students to talk *while* they demonstrate. They will depend too much on their visual aids if you let them. This is a speech.

Evaluation
1. You may evaluate the written outlines.
2. Use the Demonstration Speech Scoring Guide to evaluate the speeches.

Demonstration Speech Assignment Sheet

You will be making a 3–5 minute speech incorporating visual aids to demonstrate how something is done. A demonstration speech allows you to show a step-by-step process, such as how to play a game or accomplish a procedure.

Complete the following steps:
1. Choose your topic. Make sure it is something you know about that will interest the class. Be sure that you choose a topic you can demonstrate in the classroom.
2. Outline your speech
   - Introduce your speech to grab the audience's attention and make clear how their lives will be improved by learning this.
   - Construct the body of the speech so that the steps are listed in order.
   - Conclude your speech by restating your main points and tying up your ideas.
   - The outline must be typed or written in blue or black ink in the proper form and must be submitted prior to speech. For a 3–5 minute speech, you'll need a solid two-page outline. Avoid complete sentences since you will be tempted to memorize them.
3. You must incorporate visual aids in your presentation. (See Using Visual Aids.) You may use pictures, posters, audio aids, objects, etc. Do not use video tapes or slides.
   - Practice the entire speech—*aloud*—many times. Get friends and family to listen to you and give suggestions.
   - Be sure to practice using your audio/visual aids.
   - If you need help, ask for it.
   - Make an appointment with the teacher to ask questions or clarify. Do not ask to practice just for the teacher.
   - If you need another person to help you, arrange it ahead of time.
4. Your introduction and conclusion should be memorized.
5. You may use your outline when you speak; it's recommended that you transfer it to 3 x 5 cards to make it less obvious.

Sample Demonstration Outline (Basic)

Topic: Potting Succulents

Introduction: When I was born, my parents were farmers. I imagine that is one reason I have always appreciated plants. Years ago, while living in an apartment, I would save coffee cans and pick up old wood boxes so I could try growing flowers and vegetables on the patio. Most plants were annuals and died after one growing season; that was disappointing. Then, a few years ago a friend introduced me to succulents—you know, the plants that store water and need little care. Today, nearly all my potted plants are succulents. Once established, they are easy to grow—for years; but they do require that I follow specific steps in first planting them.

Body:
1. Getting the necessary materials:
   Dirt (cactus mix)
   Containers—type and size
   Wire screen
   Pebbles or small stones

2. Preparation of container

3. Placement of plant in pot

4. Fill with dirt

5. Top with stones

6. Watering:
   After a few days
   Once a week, once a month

Conclusion: So, if you wish to grow succulents successfully, remember to be sure you have the right mixture of soil, the right size pot, and the proper watering schedule.

Sample Demonstration Outline (Advanced)

Content: Cookies

Intent: To show how to make Toll House Cookies

I. **Introduction:** (pertinent question) What is America's favorite pastime? Right. Eating. And what makes really good eating is that all-time favorite: chocolate chip cookies.

II. **Thesis:** Chocolate chip cookies taste great, and are simple to make.

III. **Body:** (time)

    A. Gather equipment

        1. Bowl

        2. Spoons

        3. Cups

        4. Spatula

    B. Gather ingredients

        1. Flour (2 C)

        2. Sugar

            a) Brown (3/4 C)

            b) White (3/4 C)

        3. Butter or shortening (1 C)

        4. 1t. baking soda

        5. 1t. salt

        6. 1t. vanilla

        7. 2 eggs

        8. 12 oz. chocolate chips

    C. Make cookies

        1. In one bowl, add mix dry ingredients.

        2. In separate bowl, cream shortening and sugar.

        3. Add vanilla to wet ingredients.

        4. Add eggs to wet ingredients.

        5. Slowly add dry ingredients to wet ingredients.

        6. Mix well.

        7. Stir in chocolate chips.

        8. Drop by rounded teaspoons onto greased cookie sheet.

        9. Bake at 375 degrees for 10–12 minutes.

IV. **Conclusion:** (central point summary) Chocolate cookies are simple to make and they taste great. It's no wonder that they are America's favorite treat.

Demonstration Speech Scoring Guide

Scoring Criteria	Exceptional 5	Accomplished 4	Competent 3	Developing 2 / 1
Organization/ Wording				
introduction				
conclusion				
step-by-step process				
appropriate language				
Audio/Visual				
support of demonstra-tion				
quality of aids to be seen and heard				
Delivery				
eye contact				
gesture				
vocal variety				
posture				
Overall				
preparation and practice				
meeting time guidelines				

Expository Speech

A step-by-step guide for researching, writing, and delivering an informative speech with visual aids.

Materials

Scoring Criteria for Expository Speeches
Expository Speech General Topic Ideas
Suggestions for Expository Speeches
Expository Speech Library Research Worksheet
Expository Speech Sources for Works Cited Page
Expository Speech Outline Form
Using Visual Aids (page 74)
Expository Directed Listening
Expository Speech Peer Evaluation Form
Expository Speech Scoring Guide
Appendix 7: Warm Up Exercises (optional)

Procedure

1. Review the elements of an original speech and good speaking skills by handing out Scoring Criteria for Expository Speeches. Stress that the purpose is not to persuade but to present the "perfect" lecture. Tell the students that their goal is to inform and entertain their audience so that it will listen, understand and remember the information they give. Tell them that an expository speech will:
   - Tell us about a process, a person or an item
   - Give us information so that we can understand the speaker's perspective
   - Entertain us enough to keep our interest, but not distract from what the speakers want to say.
2. Tell the students that they will be speaking 4–6 minutes on a topic of their choice. Distribute and review Expository Speech General Topic Ideas. Ask them to choose a topic and begin gathering sources of information. They may choose a subject or demonstrate a process.
3. Inform the students that they will be required to use three citations from three different published sources, with evidence quoted word-for-word. Distribute the Expository Speech Library Research Worksheet and the Expository Speech Sources for Works Cited Page and review. Allow 2–3 days for library research.
4. Distribute the Expository Speech Outline Form, review outlining procedures, and have the students outline their speeches. If necessary, facilitate Scrambled Outline of a Speech on page 68.
5. Pass out Using Visual Aids and remind students that visual aids must enhance—not dominate—their presentations.
6. Ask students to submit a draft outline of their speech, complete with a works cited page that demonstrates which sources they used. Stress that they must use correct citation procedures.
7. Once you have approved the drafts, distribute the Scoring Criteria for Expository Speeches and review.
8. Divide the students into pairs to practice their entire speeches *aloud* several times.
9. Schedule the presentations.
10. If the speakers need invigorating, employ the warm up exercises from Appendix 7 before the speeches begin.

Teacher Tips

Instead of dividing the class into pairs, you may assign students to have friends and family listen to them and complete the Expository Directed Listening.

Evaluation

1. You may wish to grade the final outlines.
2. Use the Expository Speech Peer Evaluation Form for students to assess each other.
3. The Expository Speech Scoring Guide is for teacher use.

Note: All of the evaluative tools are based on the elements of the Scoring Criteria for Expository Speeches.

Scoring Criteria for Expository Speeches

Scoring Criteria	Exceptional 5	Accomplished 4	Competent 3	Developing 2 / 1
Structural/ Organizational Conventions Introduction Main Ideas Conclusion	• Cleaver attention getter. • Clear, imaginative thesis and preview. • Main ideas equal and separate with ample support material. • Ideas connected by original transitions, logical throughout; creative pattern.	• Attention getter, clear thesis and preview. • Main ideas support thesis • Support material is appropriate. • Organizational pattern is clear. • Transitions are clear and appropriate. • Conclusion summarizes, ties to introduction, and leaves audience with a final thought.	• Introduction used, but may not lead smoothly to thesis. • Thesis is clear, but may be worded incorrectly. • Main points may not be worded clearly, but organization is apparent. • Uses a conclusion that summarizes.	• States topic as introduction or begins with thesis. • No clear organizational pattern; rambling comments lack structure. • Expresses many unsupported opinions and/or adds quoted material randomly. • Conclusion brief, undeveloped; "Well, that's it."
Structural/ Organizational Conventions Supporting materials	• Quoted material is used selectively. • Quoted material is used creatively and appropriately. • Quoted material is cited correctly. • Sophisticated transitions into and out of quoted material. • Research material comes from a wide variety of quality sources.	• Quoted material is used appropriately, but may not be selective. • Quoted material is cited correctly. • Functional transitions into and out of quoted material. • Research material comes from a limited variety of quality sources.	• Quoted material is used, but may be too general or inappropriate. • Citations may be incomplete. • Transitions may be incomplete or poorly worded. • Research material comes from a limited variety of sources that do not meet requirements.	• Quoted material is not used. • Citations are not given • Transitions may be missing or poorly worded. • Research material comes from only one or two sources or sources of poor quality.
Appropriateness of Content/ Language for audience for purpose for assignment	• Speaker has obviously considered the audience. • Examples and words are creative and well-chosen. • Well-chosen "trivia" enhances the speech. • Speaker displays a clear understanding of assignment and purpose.	• Speaker makes limited use of knowledge of audience. • Speaker attempts to appeal to common experience of audience. • Some "trivia" is added to speech for interest. • Speaker meets requirements of assignment.	• Speaker makes limited adjustment to audience. • Little attempt to add interesting "trivia." • Basic compliance with requirements of assignment.	• No adjustment to audience. • Strays from assignment. • Stays only with basic information. • Makes inappropriate comments. • Uses slang or inappropriate language.

Scoring Criteria for Expository Speeches, continued.

Scoring Criteria	Exceptional 5	Accomplished 4	Competent 3	Developing 2 / 1
Physical Expression Eye contact Posture Gesture Movement	• Strong eye contact with entire audience. • Posture is strong, commanding, and purposeful. • Gestures and movement are natural and effective.	• Sustains eye contact with audience. • Stands with purpose. • Uses some gestures and movement to enhance message. • Exhibits some nervous behavior.	• Eye contact is sporadic; speaker may look at only one part of audience or may use notes frequently. • Uses few gestures and limited or no movement. • Exhibits frequent and/or repetitive nervous behavior.	• Avoids eye contact; may read from notes or rarely glance at audience. • May slouch or stand off balance. • May be stiff. • Gestures/ movement are inappropriate, nervous, stiff, or nonexistent.
Vocal Expression Rate too fast/slow Volume too loud/soft Pitch too high/low Articulation/ pronunciation.	• Speaker is enjoyable to hear, uses expression and emphasis. • Tone is conversational, but with purpose. • Voice sounds natural, neither patterned nor monotone. • Speaker pronounces words clearly and correctly.	• Speaker speaks clearly, using expression. • Conversational style is evident, but spontaneity may be lacking. • Speaker's pace and volume make speech easy to listen to and understand.	• Speaker may lack spontaneity and/or conversational style. A vocal pattern or monotone may be apparent. • Volume may be too soft or rate too fast.	• Speaker makes little attempt to use vocal techniques to communicate. • Displays a variety of weaknesses: monotone, soft volume, hesitation, verbal "fillers" (uh, um, y'know), giggling.
Visual/Aids Integration Amplification of message Clarity/Quality	• Speaker integrates a variety of objects, charts, graphs, etc. • Aids are used creatively to amplify the message. • Materials used are quality products, vivid, simple, easy to see, hear, and understand.	• Speaker uses some objects, charts, graphs, etc., while others are merely decorative. • Sometimes use does not enhance message. • Materials used are quality products, easy to see, hear.	• Speaker displays some objects, charts, graphs, etc., but relationship to content of speech may not be clear. • Quality may be inconsistent.	• Speaker uses insufficient aids or misuses aids. • Aids are of poor quality. • Aids do not enhance message.
Overall Impact Energy Enthusiasm Sincerity Originality/ creativity	• Speaker appears to have strong interest in topic. • Speaker demonstrates desire to have the audience listen, understand, and remember. • Overall presentation is creative and exciting.	• Speaker appears to have some interest in topic. • Speaker is well-prepared, displaying confident control of information. • Speaker makes clear attempt to communicate with audience.	• Speaker displays good preparation, but may lack confidence and enthusiasm. • Speaker speaks more to fulfill assignment than to communicate with audience.	• Speaker creates impression of being inadequately prepared. • Speaker lacks confidence and enthusiasm. • Little attempt to communicate effectively with audience.

Expository Speech General Topic Ideas

1. A simple subject like spiders, bananas, chocolate, the Ninja, the Air Force, cereal . . .

2. Diseases like epilepsy, diabetes, alcoholism or mental diseases like schizophrenia, depression, and anorexia.

   Connections: Some biology teachers require an expository speech about communicable diseases. Check with your biology teacher. If you've already done your biology presentation, you can revise it and use it for this class. Check with your history teacher about possible similar connections related to decade projects.

3. Scientific topics like fusion, fission or hydroponics.

4. Active hobbies like hang-gliding, snowboarding or training dogs.

5. Arts or crafts like origami, juggling, tie dying, and karate.

6. Collections like baseball cards, stamps, and comic books.

7. Humanistic topics like handwriting analysis, astrology, and color analysis.

8. Defining or describing topics like "three types of child abuse" or "thrash-funk music."

9. A tradition or practice from your culture.

   Connections: Some foreign language classes will require a cultural history unit. Check with the teacher to save time and use this class in the most practical of ways.

10. A famous person or an historical event.

    Connections: This topic may also apply to other classes. Check with your history or social studies teacher.

Suggestions for Expository Speeches

ADD
Aircraft Carrier
Alcoholism
Alphabet
Astrology
Athletic shoes
Barbie
Baseball
Baseball card collecting
Basques
Beatles
Blue jeans
Cancer
Charlie Chaplin
Chicken pox
China
China-Japan Wars
Chinese foot binding
Coffee
Cold Fusion
Competition/Horses
Credit cards
Crocodilians
Cross-country skiing
Crucifixion
Cults
Cystic fibrosis
Dance (tap)
Dolphins

Dragons
Dream interpretation
Eagles (the bird, not the group)
ESP
Extra-terrestrials
Fingers
Flying squirrels
Frisbees
Ghosts
Golf
Graphology
Halloween
Horse racing
Jackie Robinson
Jim Morrison
Kidnapping
KKK
Magic Johnson
Marilyn Monroe
Marriage Customs
Mike Jordan
Multiple Personality Disorders
Nostradamus
Optical illusion
Pizza
Plastic
Poisons

POWs
Religious practices
Ronnie Lott
Samurai
Sea Urchins
SETI
Sharks
Sixties Revolution
Skis
Sleep
Space stations
Sports injuries
Sports violence
Stress
Subliminal messages
Sumo
Superstitions
Symbolism of apples
Teddy bears
Tofu
Vampires/Dracula
Video games
Volcanoes
Walt Disney
Will Clark
Winchester House
Unsolved mysteries
Wombats
Yo-yo

Expository Speech Library Research Worksheet

Name_____

Due: End of Day #1 in the Library

Directions: Write down what information you were able to find on your proposed topic. Indicate what pages you will use and what visual aids might be possible from the information you gathered.

Do not worry about the introduction and conclusion at this point.

You may wish to check out books today on your topic or make photocopies of the articles you will wish to use in the construction of your outline.

1. Topic: _____
   Thesis: _____
   _____
   _____

2. Source #1: (Use Form Attached)

   Main Point Supported By This Evidence:

   Possible Visual Aid:

3. Source #2 (Use Form Attached)

   Main Point Supported By This Evidence:

   Possible Visual Aid:

4. Source #3 (Use Form Attached)

   Main Point Supported By This Evidence:

   Possible Visual Aid:

5. Source #4 (Use Form Attached)

   Main Point Supported By This Evidence:

   Possible Visual Aid:

6. Souce #5 (Use Form Attached)

   Main Point Supported By This Evidence:

   Possible Visual Aid(s):

Name_____

Due: End of Day #2 in the Library

Referring to the sources you found in your search yesterday, begin identifying material you will use in your speech. What major subtopics do you wish to include? Most often used categories might include:

• History/background
• Importance of subject to audience
• Parts, ingredients, equipment necessary, terminology
• Use/variations/applications
• Future modifications
• Pertinent addresses or contact information

Check each Table of Contents at the beginning of your sources for hints on how to organize your topic.

Spend some time reading from the sources you found yesterday. Construct a rough draft outline for the *body* of your speech. Cite sources you will use to support each section. Refer to the sample below:

Sample Outline

   I. The Grand Canyon
      A. Vital Statistics (Hielman, Walter C. *The Mystery of Erosion*. Boulder: Colorado Press, 1999)
         1. Location
         2. Dimensions
         3. History
      B. Wildlife (Thomas, Sid. *Wildlife of an Ancient Canyon*. Tempe: Arizona State Press Association, 1995)
         1. Birds
         2. Fish
         3. Reptiles (snakes, etc.)
         4. Other animals who "visit"
      C. Recreation/visitation ("Arizona Travel." Phoenix: Arizona Travel Bureau Pamphlet, 1995)
         1. Packing

2. Rafting ("Whitewater on a Budget." Boulder: Colorado Travel Association, 1999)

3. Climbing

4. Air passage/tours ("Uncle Terry Tours of the Canyon." *ABC Tour Books—Colorado/Arizona*. Chicago: ABC Press, 1999)

D. Future Preservation ("Friends of the Canyon". *TIME* November 6, 1998: 45–47)

1. Colorado River

2. Future erosion

3. Air pollution

4. Damage from tourism

5. Impact of pollution

Expository Speech Sources for Works Cited Page

- Fill out source requirements completely. Five must be found and used; only three need to be quoted in the speech.
- Write "none listed" if an author's name or copyright date is not listed.

1. Author's name _____

   Title of book, magazine, or website used _____

   Title of article in above book or magazine _____

   Chapter and/or pages read_____ Date of above publication_____

2. Author's name _____

   Title of book, magazine, or website used _____

   Title of article in above book or magazine _____

   Chapter and/or pages read_____ Date of above publication_____

3. Author's name _____

   Title of book, magazine, or website used _____

   Title of article in above book or magazine _____

   Chapter and/or pages read_____ Date of above publication_____

4. Author's name _____

   Title of book, magazine, or website used _____

   Title of article in above book or magazine _____

   Chapter and/or pages read_____ Date of above publication_____

5. Author's name _____

   Title of book, magazine, or website used _____

   Title of article in above book or magazine _____

   Chapter and/or pages read_____ Date of above publication_____

Interview Sources

1. Person interviewed_____ Date of interview _____

   His position, occupation, and location _____

   Why is he a reliable source? Be specific _____

2. Person interviewed_____ Date of interview _____

   His position, occupation, and location _____

   Why is he a reliable source? Be specific _____

3. Person interviewed_____ Date of interview _____

   His position, occupation, and location _____

   Why is he a reliable source? Be specific _____

Personal Experience of Speaker

1. Tell (1) when, (2) where, and (3) conditions under which you became an authority on subject matter in your speech.

Expository Speech Outline Form

Name_____

Construct a neat, complete-sentence outline.

Content: _____

Intent _____

_____

Number of words in outline:_____ Date: _____

   I. **Introduction:**

    II. **Thesis:**

    III. **Body:** (Note Where Evidence Cards and Visuals Will Be Used)

    III. **Conclusion:**

- Instructor's comments may concern choice of topic, development of ideas, organization, language use, personal appearance, posture, physical activity, sources, and improvement.

Expository Directed Listening

Directions: This is an exercise designed to measure your listening and comprehension skills. Carefully listen to each speech, filling out this form as you listen or after you listen. Do not share your information with anyone else.

Speech Content: _____

I. The thesis sentence: _____

_____

II. Three of the main points/the type of support used (example, statistic, fact)

A. _____

  1. _____

B. _____

  1. _____

C. _____

  1. _____

III. One thing the speaker did that made the speech entertaining/memorable _____

_____

_____

Expository Speech Peer Evaluation Form

Name of Speaker _____

Please indicate   1=got it!   2=almost   3=say what?

_____ eye contact   I especially liked _____

_____ preparation   _____

_____ rate of speaking   _____

_____ imagination   To improve your next speech I suggest that you _____

_____ volume   _____

_____ acceptable grammar   _____

_____ posture and poise   _____

Name of Speaker _____

Please indicate   1=got it!   2=almost   3=say what?

_____ eye contact   I especially liked _____

_____ preparation   _____

_____ rate of speaking   _____

_____ imagination   To improve your next speech I suggest that you _____

_____ volume   _____

_____ acceptable grammar   _____

_____ posture and poise   _____

Name of Speaker _____

Please indicate   1=got it!   2=almost   3=say what?

_____ eye contact   I especially liked _____

_____ preparation   _____

_____ rate of speaking   _____

_____ imagination   To improve your next speech I suggest that you _____

_____ volume   _____

_____ acceptable grammar   _____

_____ posture and poise   _____

Expository Speech Scoring Guide

	Exceptional 5	Accomplished 4	Competent 3	Developing 2 / 1
Structural/Organizational Conventions				
Introduction				
Main Ideas				
Conclusion				
Structural/Organizational Conventions				
Supporting Materials				
Appropriateness of Content/ Language				
for audience				
for purpose				
for assignment				
Physical Expression				
Eye contact				
Posture				
Gesture				
Movement				
Vocal Expression				
Rate too fast/slow				
Volume too loud/soft				
Pitch too high/low				
Articulation/pronunciation				
Visual/Aids				
Integration				
Amplification of message				
Clarity/Quality				
Overall Impact				
Energy				
Enthusiasm				
Sincerity				
Originality/creativity				

Comments:

Recommendations:

103

SECTION IV
Persuasive Speaking

We are bombarded by persuasion daily. This section encourages students to be aware of persuasive techniques and teaches them how to implement elements of persuasion to convince the audience to change its beliefs or to take action.

The Sales Pitch

A sales presentation that demonstrates special persuasive techniques.

Materials

Sales Pitch Summary Sheet
Sales Pitch Advertisement Form
Literary Sales Pitch Advertisement Form
Product Sales Pitch Scoring Guide
Literary Sales Pitch Scoring Guide

Procedure

You can ask the class to pitch either a product or a literary work.

Product

1. Ask the class to choose a product they would like to promote. The students can pick one currently on the market or design one of their own. Make sure that the product is class-appropriate—no alcohol or tobacco.
2. Tell the students that they are to develop a 2–3 minute sales pitch that will convince a panel of three students to advertise their product.
3. Distribute the Sales Pitch Summary Sheet and review it with the class. Also review the evaluation criteria.
4. Hand out copies of Sales Pitch Advertisement Form and tell the students to use it in preparing their pitches.
5. Select the panel members who will judge the pitches and schedule the presentations.
6. If the speakers need invigorating, employ the warm up exercises from Appendix 7.

Literary Work

1. Tell the class that they will be literary agents, trying to get an editorial board to accept a piece for inclusion in an anthology.
2. Ask the students to select a poem, essay, speech or excerpt of a novel or short story they would want to include.
3. Distribute the Sales Pitch Summary Sheet and review it with the class. Also review the evaluation criteria.
4. Hand out copies of the Literary Sales Pitch Advertisement Form and tell the students to use it in preparing their pitches.
5. Select the members of the editorial board and schedule the presentations.

Teacher Tips

1. To add another dimension of skill level to the literary sales pitch, you may ask students to provide an oral interpretation of an excerpt from their chosen selection that develops a tone consistent with the argument being made for the piece's inclusion (e.g., if they're advocating that a poem be placed in the "modern anxiety" section of your text, it shouldn't be read with an inspirational tone).
2. Once the panels have approved the presentations, you may ask the students to prepare their live or video advertisements.

Evaluation

Use the Product Sales Pitch Scoring Guide or the Literary Sales Pitch Scoring Guide.

Sales Pitch Summary Sheet

The Direct Approach

Use a direct approach when your audience is receptive to your ideas. This persuasive technique allows you to present your ideas at once.

Here's how:

- Open with a hook to catch the audience's attention.
  Hook: Provide a brief (1-minute) motivation to grab your audience.

- In the body, provide a list of reasons people should act on your ideas.
  List: Give the audience the information they need to support your idea. Include specific reasons why your idea/product is worth their support. Don't stint on details. Remember: "The more you tell, the more you sell."

- Finish by giving the audience a handle, or tell them what to do and why they should act fast.
  Handle: Make the action sound easy. Give the audience a positive reason for supporting your idea. Avoid "if" and "why not" closes. They lack positive emphasis and encourage your listener to say, "So?"

The Indirect Approach

Use an indirect approach when your audience is not receptive to your ideas. This persuasive technique allows you to dine with your opposition before selling them the product.

Here's how:

- Open with a hook that acknowledges something bad about the product.
  Hook: Provide a brief motivation to grab your audience. (e.g., Yuck! There's no denying that we've all tasted cough medicine that's more delicious than this. But is it more effective? . . .)

- In the body provide a list of reasons people should act on your ideas.
  List: Give the audience the information they need to support your idea. Include specific reasons why your idea/product is worth their support despite its negative qualities. Don't stint on details. Remember: "The more you tell, the more you sell."

- Finish by giving the audience a handle, or tell them what to do and why they should act fast.
  Handle: Make the action sound easy. Give the audience a positive reason for supporting your idea. It's OK to remind them about the product's negative quality, but always end with a positive reason why they should buy your product. (e. g. "Brand x cough syrup may not taste great; but it will work better than any of that sweet stuff.")

Sales Pitch Advertisement Form

Advertisements begin _____

Fill in the following information for each ad:

Who: **When:**

What: **Why:**

Where: **How:**

Target Age Group:

On which type of radio or TV station should your advertisement be played?

How will your advertisement catch people's attention?

How will you make your product look attractive to your customers?

Literary Sales Pitch Assignment Form

1. Chose a piece of literature poem—short story, essay, speech, play, novel excerpt—for inclusion in your anthology, and pitch it to an editorial board in a 4–5 minute presentation.

2. The order of your presentation is up to you, but you must prepare a focused sales pitch that:
   - clearly states the author, title and genre of the selection
   - addresses WHY this piece of lit needs to be included in the anthology
   - reveals where it should be placed in the anthology and why
   - creatively engages the audience to "buy" your idea

Product Sales Pitch Scoring Guide

	Excellent	Good	Fair	Poor	Comments
Clearly states the intended audience of the product	5	4	3	2 / 1	
Addresses why the product should be purchased	5	4	3	2 / 1	
Reveals where the add should be placed and why	5	4	3	2 / 1	
Creatively engages the audience	5	4	3	2 / 1	
Presents a clear, creative structure	5	4	3	2 / 1	
Stays within the time limit	5	4	3	2 / 1	

Literary Sales Pitch Scoring Guide

	Excellent	Good	Fair	Poor	Comments
Clearly states the author, title and genre of the selection	5	4	3	2 / 1	
Addresses why the piece should be included	5	4	3	2 / 1	
Reveals where it should be placed and why	5	4	3	2 / 1	
Creatively engages the audience	5	4	3	2 / 1	
Presents a clear, creative structure	5	4	3	2 / 1	
Stays within the time limit	5	4	3	2 / 1	

Surplus Sales

A 2–4 minute speech encouraging the real-world application of persuasion.

Materials
Monopoly® money
Surplus Sales Assignment Sheet
Product Sales Pitch Scoring Guide (page 111)
Appendix 7: Warm Up Exercises (optional)

Procedure
Whether standing in a used car lot, getting that telemarketer call during dinner, or tuning in for a late night "infomercial," we will all be victims or beneficiaries of the sales "pitch" that plays off of our desires rather than our needs. By allowing students to create these spurious arguments, they will be more likely to recognize a huckster's strategies and become more critical consumers.

1. Tell students that they are to select a product to sell to their classmates. This is a permanent sale. They will not be able to retain the product.
2. Encourage students to select an item that is not of great monetary or sentimental value. Often, a unique item will be more popular than something that is new. No tobacco, alcohol or live animals may be sold.
3. Give students a copy of the Surplus Sales Assignment Sheet, They can construct their sales pitches in class or at home for homework.
4. Have students sign up for a speaking day.
5. On the day of the sales, distribute Monopoly® money for bidding. No other currency will be exchanged. Each person will get the same amount at the beginning. No pooling of cash is allowed!
6. If the speakers need invigorating, employ the warm up exercises from Appendix 7.
7. You or another student can act as the onsite auctioneer. Be prepared to offer a minimum price suggestion, "I'd like to start bidding at . . ."
8. Following the pitches, debrief with the students on which pitches they fell for and why. Emphasize the fact that all of the products sold were bought out of desire not need. Encourage them to make parallels between this experience and advertisements that they encounter regularly.

Evaluation
1. Use the Product Sales Pitch Scoring Guide on p. 111
2. You can give extra credit or perks to the students who fetched the highest price for their products.

Surplus Sales Assignment Sheet

The Selection

This is a permanent sale. You will not be able to retain the product.

Select an item that is not of great monetary or sentimental value.

Often, a unique item will be more popular than something that is new.

No live animals or people may be sold.

The Process

1. Introduction—"Get their attention!" The introduction techniques you use in expository speeches will work here too. Remember that you will want to begin developing a rapport with your audience immediately! Begin by letting your audience know that you "understand their pain" and/or let them know why you are the expert.

2. Create a need—Any good salesman will paint a picture of doom and gloom and then will present the product as the panacea. Paint a picture. Imagine a world without your product. Don't limit your pitch to "wants." Your audience must need your product!

3. Describe the product—Although you may want to create a "mystery product," you will want to point out the strengths of your product. Describe its convenience, beauty, value, and its inexpensive nature.

4. Techniques— Perhaps some of these ideas will be useful. Certainly, there is no end to the techniques used to sell us items in our society.
   - Offer us an "offer we can't refuse."
   - Create an element of mystery.
   - Don't overlook the benefits of bonus gifts for early purchase.
   - Suggest we act early because of demand.
   - More, more, more—watch "Home Shopping Network," commercials, and infomercials.

Bidding/Sales

- At the onset of the sales, each student will be given an equal amount of Monopoly® money.
- We will have an on-site auctioneer! Be prepared to offer a minimum price suggestion, "I'd like to start bidding at . . ."
- You may at any time jump up and resell something you have already bought for extra credit.
- If time allows, you may split or modify any package and sell all or a portion of your purchases.

Speech to Persuade

An activity teaching students how to design a speech to convince an audience to change beliefs or to take action.

Materials

Speech to Persuade: Logos, Ethos, Pathos (teacher edition)

Speech to Persuade: Logos, Ethos, Pathos (student edition)

Persuasive Writing Style

Suggested Topics for the Persuasive Speech

Speech to Persuade Assignment Sheet

Persuasive Speech Sources for Works Cited Page

Persuasive Speech Outline

Persuasive Speech Sample Outlines 1 & 2

Scoring Criteria for Persuasive Speeches

Persuasive Speech Evaluation Form

Scoring Guide for Persuasive Speeches

Persuasive Audience Attitude Survey

Appendix 10: Sample Persuasive Speech with MLA Documentation (optional)

Procedure

1. Tell your students that they will be making speeches designed to persuade. Distribute Speech to Persuade: Logos, Ethos, Pathos, and Persuasive Writing Style. Review the elements of persuasive speaking.

2. Ask the students to select a controversial proposition that describes a course of action they want taken. Emphasize that the topic must be controversial, not one on which all students can agree. You may want to distribute and review Suggested Topics for the Persuasive Speech if the students have difficulty finding a topic.

3. Hand out the Speech to Persuade Assignment Sheet and review carefully.

4. Distribute the Persuasive Speech Sources for Works Cited Page. Tell the students that these speeches will require research, and review research and proper citation procedure.

5. Distribute Persuasive Speech Outline and the sample outlines. Review outlining procedure.

6. Ask the students to develop their outlines following the procedure on the assignment sheet and submit them (with their bibliographies attached) to you for evaluation.

7. Once you have accepted the outlines, distribute Scoring Criteria for Persuasive Speeches and review.

8. If you are planning to have them write up a final copy of their speech, see Appendix 10: Sample Persuasive Speech with MLA Documentation.

9. Divide the class into pairs and have each pair practice its speeches—ALOUD—several times.

10. Schedule presentations. Once speakers are finished, remind them to submit their evidence cards.

Evaluation

1. You may evaluate the outlines for choice of topic, development of ideas, evidence, organization and language use.

2. You can have students evaluate each other using the Persuasive Speech Evaluation Form.

3. To assess the presentations, you can use the Scoring Guide for Persuasive Speeches. This scoring guide is based on the detailed Scoring Criteria for Persuasion Speeches.

Teacher Tips

1. Persuasive speaking and writing is difficult. You may want to revisit this activity several times—emphasizing different criteria and increasing your expectations for both delivery and content.

2. Prior to writing their outlines, students could utilize the Persuasion Audience Attitude Survey to better assess which strategies to use in their outlines.

Speech to Persuade: Logos, Ethos, Pathos
(teacher edition)

Logical Appeals: the speaker offers organized, clearly defined points; there is solid reasoning and valid evidence.
- Wouldn't my driving be more convenient than your having to drive me everywhere?
- I could help you with the errands!
- There would be less chaos at home with people rushing to drive everywhere.
- I could learn to follow directions.
- I have done well in Driver's Education. The school and state believe that I am a good driver.
- I have checked it out, and the insurance would not go up much.
- The new car would be less likely to have engine problems.
- I'll pay for my own gas and insurance, plus I will keep the car clean.
- I'll be sure to call you when I get where I am going.

Emotional Appeals: the speaker's words arouse feelings in the audience like anger, disgust, compassion, etc.
- When you were a kid, didn't you want to be given responsibility, too?
- Will you consider my driving if I ask only on special occasions? You know how special some things can be, don't you?
- If I'm driving, you don't have to worry about my being in a car when the driver has been drinking.
- I would feel so proud for others to see me in our new car!
- I would never ask if I thought you didn't trust me.
- How would you feel always having to bum a ride with people?
- I would love the responsibility!
- I know that you worry about me, so out of respect for you two, I would be extra careful.
- I would love you guys so much!
- This would really enhance my self-esteem.
- Think what this could do for our communication. We would talk more and understand each other better!

Personal Appeals: the speaker wins the audience's trust through honesty, competency, and credibility. The listeners will buy what you are selling because they trust in you and your credibility—your believability
- I promise to always tell you the truth about where I am going.
- I don't feel that it is always right that my friends always have to drive.

- Since my sister was allowed to drive a nice car when she first got her license, I think that this would be the fair thing to do, don't you?
- Please don't judge me before I have had a chance to prove to you that I can handle this.
- Have I ever let you down? I mean, when it really counts?
- I would like to show you that I can be as disciplined with a car as I have been with my life.
- I give you my word that I will be a good and responsible driver.

Speech to Persuade: Logos, Ethos, Pathos
(student edition)

Logical Appeals: the speaker offers organized, clearly defined points; there is solid reasoning and valid evidence.

Emotional Appeals: the speaker's words arouse feelings in the audience like anger, disgust, compassion, etc

Personal Appeals: the speaker wins the audience's trust through honesty, competency, and credibility. The listeners will buy what you are selling because they trust in you and your credibility—your believability.

The following are possible answers to the question: "If you had just received your driver's license, what would you say to your parents to persuade them to allow you to drive the family's brand new car?"

Determine whether you think each appeal is Logical (L), Emotional (E) or Personal (P). Mark your choice next to each answer.

_____ There would be less chaos at home with people rushing to drive everywhere.

_____ I would never ask, if I thought you didn't trust me.

_____ How would you feel always having to bum a ride with people?

_____ The new car would be less likely to have engine problems.

_____ Please don't judge me before I have had a chance to prove to you that I can handle this.

_____ I'll be sure to call you when I get where I am going.

_____ This would really enhance my self-esteem.

_____ I promise to always tell you the truth about where I am going.

_____ I have checked it out, and the insurance would not go up much.

_____ When you were a kid, didn't you want to be given responsibility, too?

_____ Since my sister was allowed to drive a nice car when she first got her license, I think that this would be the fair thing to do, don't you?

_____ Will you consider my driving if I ask only on special occasions? You know how *special* some things can be, don't you?

_____ If I'm driving, you don't have to worry about my being in a car when the driver has been drinking.

_____ I don't feel that it is right that my friends always have to drive.

_____ I would feel so proud for others to see me in our new car!

_____ I could help you with the errands!

_____ I would like to show you that I can be as disciplined with a car as I have been with my life.

_____ I could learn to follow directions.

_____ Wouldn't my driving be more convenient than your having to drive me every-where?

_____ I would love the responsibility!

_____ I know that you worry about me, so out of respect for you, I will be extra careful.

_____ I give you my word that I will be a good and responsible driver.

_____ Think what this could do for our communication. We would talk more and under-stand each other better!

_____ I'll pay for my own gas and insurance, plus I will keep the car clean.

_____ I would love you guys so much!

_____ I have done well in Driver's Education. The school and state believe that I am a good driver.

_____ Have I ever let you down? I mean, when it really counts?

Persuasive Writing Style

Persuasive writing style may include:

Allusion: Famous personages, or myth. An allusion can be used in isolation or as an extension that holds an entire oration together. The image chosen often tells an entire story in and of itself.

Analogy: Comparison made between something unfamiliar and something familiar. Abstract ideas can be made much more understandable through comparisons with something more familiar.

Example: An instance, a happening, and a measurable, quantifiable event in time. Be careful that one example is not being used to constitute truth.

Illustration: A story used to demonstrate an idea or to make a point. While the illustration may be based upon a true story that happened at some point in time, illustrations can never be used to substantiate proof.

Imagery: Word pictures that often take on a deeper, symbolic meaning.

Irony: Actual intent expressed in words that carry the opposite meaning. Irony is not as harsh in language as sarcasm is; yet its effect is more cutting because of its indirect nature. It is characterized by a grim humor, a detachment on the part of the writer.

Paradox: Two directly contradictory images/concepts used together. Truth is found somewhere between the two contradictory ideas. Charles Dickens' *Tale of Two Cities* beautifully illustrates paradox in its opening paragraph: "It was the best of times; it was the worst of times. It was the age of wisdom; it was the age of foolishness. It was the spring of hope; it was the winter of despair."

Parallel Structure: Repeated use of the same grammatical structure for emphasis. The speeches of John F. Kennedy serve as effective examples of parallel structure.

Refrain: A statement repeated at different transitional points during the oration. The statement usually will be symbolic in its content.

Repetition: A restatement of a phrase or words. Although effective, overuse may turn into tongue-in-cheek, satire or irony.

Satire: A critical attitude blended with humor. Satire gently "pokes fun at our human foibles."

Suggested Topics for the Persuasive Speech

1. Any juvenile convicted of an adult crime should receive the same penalty under the law as an adult.
2. Income taxes are an unfair penalty that hurts individuals who work hard and stimulate the economy.
3. Parents should not be able to regulate reading material chosen for students by educational professionals.
4. Television, Internet access, and video games influence children in negative ways.
5. Students benefit by a school day that begins later, because of increased sleep time.
6. Hormones and drugs given to animals for fast growth must be stopped.
7. The right to keep and bear arms has been grossly and carelessly administered.
8. Freedom of speech is our most valued constitutional right.
9. Terminally ill individuals should have the right to choose the time and nature of their death, if death is irreversibly imminent.
10. The Right to Bear Arms is not an absolute constitutional right and therefore, the ownership of guns can justifiably be controlled.
11. Civil disobedience, whether violent or nonviolent, is a necessary aspect of our democracy and must be protected as an absolute right.
12. Creationism should be taught in the public schools as an alternative.
13. Affirmative Action has outlived its usefulness and has become counter-productive.
14. The teen media is largely responsible for the moral degradation of teenagers.
15. Professional athletes are paid too much.
16. Rating CDs is an ineffective method of protecting children.
17. Children of homeless individuals should be removed from their parents and put in the protective custody of the state.
18. The Right to Privacy seriously impacts gun safety, allowing high-risk individuals to own guns and use them irresponsibly.
19. Biomedical technology is too dangerous to pursue as a legitimate method of preventing illness.
20. The potential harms of genetic engineering far outweigh its potential benefits.
21. The potential benefits of genetic engineering far surpass its potential harms.
22. Music should be part of the required list of core classes.
23. Cloning is a necessary progression in medical science and should be fully legalized and funded by the government.
24. Curfew laws unfairly and unconstitutionally restrict the freedom of U.S. citizens.
25. Standardized tests accurately measure the strength of a school and the academic proficiency of particular students.

26. Marriage should be legally defined as the union between two people, regardless of their gender.
27. Gun registration is a violation of constitutional rights.
28. It should be permissible for women to lead and/or participate in every level of military participation, even across combat lines.
29. Abstinence is a serious commitment that all single persons should make to avoid future problems and consequences.

Speech to Persuade Assignment Sheet

1. **Select** a controversial proposition that describes a course of action you want taken. The topic should be of interest to you and your audience, and it should be one on which you can easily obtain source material. Be sure your proposition is controversial. Avoid a topic that your audience already agrees on, such as, *"We should all drive safely."* Instead, choose a debatable statement such as *"National requirements for teen drivers' licenses should be established."* State your proposition so that it contains the word "should," meaning the course of action you favor "ought to be" done.

2. **Research** the topic by interviewing authorities, making your own observations, and reading magazines and books. Get specific examples, illustrations, statistics, testimony, etc. Research until you are well informed using at least five sources. Prepare a Works Cited Page before outlining your speech.

3. **Organize** your material by including the following information in your basic organization formula:

Introduction
- **Capture:** Immediately focus attention on some aspect of your proposition.
- **Motivate:** Make your audience want to listen by describing *a problem that exists* and how this problem directly affects them. Speak from the viewpoint of the audience. Show how the problem endangers them. Tell its size and implications.
- **Assert:** Briefly state your exact proposition, which is the *solution* to the problem you have just described.
- **Preview:** Give an initial summary of your main points, indicating to your audience the ideas they should listen for.

Body
- **Point One and support:** Give *details* of your solution. What specifically is the plan? What are the rules? Who will administer them? Use concrete verbal support.
- **Point Two and support:** Show that this plan is *practical*, that it will work. Has it worked in other places: specifically, give examples. Are there safeguards for making it work? Tell them. Will it do what you say it will do? Give examples, testimony, and statistics.
- **Point Three and support:** Show that this plan is *desirable*, that it will benefit the audience.

Conclusion
- **Action:** Tell the audience what they can do to promote the plan: such as write their congressman, or subscribe, amend, do, give, clean up, etc.

If you happen to be talking *against* a proposition, follow the same steps but show how the plan is not needed, not practical, and not desirable.

4. **Outline** your speech. Prepare a *75–150* word complete sentence outline using the outline sheet attached. Be sure to note the use of evidence on the outline and attach a bibliography containing at least five sources. Make sure the evidence cards follow proper form.

   Keep your main points short and direct. Use catchy words. List concrete support for each main point. Indicate in the outline where your evidence cards will be presented.

5. **Transfer** your main points to your one presentation card. Prepare your evidence cards.

6. **Rehearse** your speech aloud. Practice it many times until you are sure of your material. You may use unlimited numbers of evidence cards, but only one presentation card. As you rehearse, try to eliminate the number of words you have on this card. Do not write your whole speech on the card. Use only key words, statistics, and exact quotes on the cards. When using notes, practice holding the card high enough to see. Make no attempt to hide the note cards.

   As you prepare your speech remember the rules for the presentations:
   - **Time limits:** You must speak at least *3* minutes and you will be stopped at *5* minutes. Time violation will result in one grade penalty per minute violation.
   - **Speaking notes:** You may use one note card, no larger than 4 x 6, as well as unlimited numbers of 4 x 6 evidence cards. Evidence cards must rest on the lectern. Visual aids are optional.
   - **Sources of information:** Your presentation must contain *three* citations from *three* different published sources required, with evidence quoted word-for-word. For each source give the specific magazine, book, or website it was taken from, using appropriate citation form.

   List these on the outline form attached.

7. **Present** your speech. Show your audience that *you* are convinced by making your voice back up your words with varied force and enthusiasm, by making your body back up your words with strong, purposeful gestures and movements. Be friendly but firm in your delivery. Really try to convince your listeners that your proposition is the best one for them and society.

   After you have spoken and returned to your desk, class members will write an evaluation of your speech, using a form supplied by the teacher. You will receive these evaluations at a later date.

Persuasive Speech Sources for Works Cited Page

Fill out source requirements completely. **Five** must be found and used; only **three** need to be quoted in the speech.

Write "none listed" if an author's name or copyright date is not listed.

1. Author's name _____
   Title of book, magazine, or website used _____
   Title of article in above book or magazine_____
   Chapter and/or pages read_____ Date of publication_____

2. Author's name _____
   Title of book, magazine, or website used _____
   Title of article in above book or magazine_____
   Chapter and/or pages read_____ Date of publication_____

3. Author's name _____
   Title of book, magazine, or website used _____
   Title of article in above book or magazine_____
   Chapter and/or pages read_____ Date of publication_____

4. Author's name _____
   Title of book, magazine, or website used _____
   Title of article in above book or magazine_____
   Chapter and/or pages read_____ Date of publication_____

5. Author's name _____
   Title of book, magazine, or website used _____
   Title of article in above book or magazine_____
   Chapter and/or pages read_____ Date of publication_____

Interview Sources

1. Person interviewed_____
   Date of interview _____
   His position, occupation, and location _____
   Why he is a reliable source? Be specific _____

Personal Experience of Speaker

Tell (1) when, (2) where, and (3) conditions under which you became an authority on the subject matter in your speech.

Persuasive Speech Outline

Construct a neat, complete-sentence outline. Your teacher may wish to write criticisms of the outline and speech in the margins, prior to the delivery date.

Content _____

Intent _____

_____

Number of words in outline: _____ Date: _____

   I. **Introduction:**

   II. **Thesis:**

   III. **Body:** (Note Where Evidence Cards and Visuals Will Be Used)

   III. **Conclusion:**

Persuasive Speech
Sample Outline 1
(When audience knows nothing about proposition)

Audience: General Public
Attitude: Neutral
Content: Search Warrants
Intent: To persuade that police should need a search warrant to search people's trash.

I. **Introduction:** (Pertinent question) What do you consider private? Your house? Your car? The U.S. Supreme Court has made some startling decisions regarding the issue of privacy. (Common appeal #1) *Your house, for instance, is private and may not be searched without a warrant. Your backyard viewed with surveillance isn't. Telephone conversations are private, but the numbers you dial to begin such conversations aren't. Your car is not private, but a suitcase in your car is.* Recently, the Supreme Court struck another blow against privacy with the *Greenwood* decision. Now, the refuse of your life, your garbage, is no longer private.

II. **Thesis:** The *Greenwood* decision should be reversed for three reasons.

III. **Body:** (Reasons)

   A. Explanation of the *Greenwood* decision (Evidence #1, *Newsweek*, 1988)

   B. Reasons for reversal

   1. Inconsistency with previous Supreme Court decisions (Evidence #2, Supreme Court summary, 1988)

   2. Violation of Fourth Amendment

   a) Constitution protects (Evidence #3, *U.S. Constitution*)

   3. Garbage reveals (Common appeal #2) *Think for a moment about a time when your parents, your brother or sister, or a friend of yours looked through your things without telling you. Maybe it was a letter that was never meant to be read or even a diary. How did you feel?*

   a) Reveals financial details

   b) Reveals sexual and health behaviors/concerns

   c) Comparison to personal effects

IV. **Conclusion:** (Visualize the future) *If the Supreme Court lets stand the* Greenwood *decision,* (Emotional appeal #1) *a key tenet of our democracy is in danger of disappearing: the individual's right to privacy. Unless we want a future where the power of the authorities grows larger and larger and the zone of individual rights smaller and smaller, we must demand the repeal of the* Greenwood *decision.*

Persuasive Speech
Sample Outline 2

Audience: Adults
Assumed Attitude: Neutral to Slightly Negative
Content: Driving
Intent: To persuade that the driving age should be raised to twenty.

I. **Introduction:** (Startling statement) (Emotional appeal #1) *Your life is in serious danger. I can save you if you give me my way. If I had my way, not one teenager would be driving.*

II. **Thesis:** Teenagers should not be allowed to drive because they are involved in too many accidents and they waste gasoline with unnecessary driving.

III. **Body** (Comparative advantages):
   A. Accidents under the current system
      1. Statistics show danger. (Evidence #1, Jones, 1976) (Rational appeal #1) *These statistics mean that a small percentage of drivers cause more than half of all accidents and those drivers are all teenagers.*
      2. Insurance rates show danger. (Evidence #2, Adams, 1972) (Rational appeal #2) *Because teenagers cause 60 percent of all accidents, their rates are 60 percent higher. Even insurance companies agree that teen drivers are a dangerous risk.*
      3. CHP Survey verifies danger. (Evidence #3, Smith, 1968)
   B. Unnecessary driving under the current system (Common appeal #1) *Think about the last time you were in terrible traffic. You sat there among all those cars, stuck on the highway, wondering where everyone could possibly be going at the same time. This kind of traffic is what teenagers create at certain times in certain places just because they feel like cruising around.*
   C. Advantages under the new system
      1. Reduced accidents
      2. Lower insurance rates
      3. Reduced gridlock in certain areas

IV. **Conclusion:** (Common appeal #2) *If a man were a known killer, I have no doubt that you would want him locked up so that you and yours would be safe. Statistically, the teenage driver is equally dangerous and unpredictable.* (Emotional appeal #2) *We must raise the driving age to 20 to save not only our resources but our lives and our children's lives.*

SAMPLE EVIDENCE
Teenagers have high accident rate

Jones, J.J., Chairman of the Commission on Safe Driving
"Teen Drivers: A Menace"
Safe Driver's Review
September 1, 1976, p. 41

Teen drivers are worse than unsafe cars. Last year teen drivers, who represent only 10 percent of all drivers, caused 40 percent of the accidents and were indirectly involved in another 20 percent.

*The information on this sample evidence card is fictitious. Yours must be real.

Scoring Criteria for Persuasive Speeches

Scoring Criteria	Exceptional 5	Accomplished 4	Competent 3	Developing 2 / 1
Structural/ Organizational Conventions Introduction Main Ideas Conclusion	• Clever attention getter. • Strong thesis calling for change. • Main ideas equal and separate with ample support material. • Ideas connected by original transitions, logical throughout; creative pattern. • Conclusion makes a final call for action—leaves audience with memorable message.	• Attention getter, clear thesis and preview. • Main ideas support thesis. • Support material is appropriate. • Organizational pattern is clear. • Transitions are clear and appropriate. • Conclusion summarizes, ties to introduction and leaves audience with a final thought.	• Introduction used, but may not lead smoothly to thesis. • Thesis is clear, but may be worded incorrectly. • Main points may not be worded clearly, but organization is apparent. • Uses a conclusion that summarizes.	• States topic as introduction or begins with thesis. • No clear organizational pattern; rambling comments lack structure. • Expresses many unsupported opinions and/or adds quoted material randomly. • Conclusion brief, undeveloped; "Well, that's it."
Structural/ Organizational Conventions Supporting Materials	• Quoted material is used selectively. • Quoted material is used creatively and appropriately. • Quoted material is cited correctly. • Sophisticated transition into and out of quoted material. • Research material comes from a wide variety of quality sources.	• Quoted material is used appropriately, but may not be selective. • Quoted material is cited correctly. • Functional transitions into and out of quoted material. • Research material comes from a limited variety of quality sources.	• Quoted material is used, but may be too general or inappropriate. • Citations may be incomplete. • Transitions may be incomplete or poorly worded. • Research material comes from a limited variety of sources that do not meet requirements.	• Quoted material is not used. • Citations are not given. • Transitions may be missing or poorly worded. • Research material comes from only one or two sources or sources of poor quality.
Appropriate-ness of Content/ Language for audience for purpose for assignment	• Speaker has obviously considered the audience. • Examples and words are creative and well-chosen. • Well-chosen appeals enhance the persuasive message. • Speaker displays a clear understanding of assignment and purpose.	• Speaker makes limited use of knowledge of audience. • Speaker attempts to appeal to common experience of audience. • Some "trivia" is added to speech for interest. • Speaker meets requirements of assignment.	• Speaker makes limited adjustment to audience. • Little attempt to add interesting "trivia." • Basic compliance with requirements of assignment.	• No adjustment to audience. Strays from assignment. • Stays only with basic information. • Makes inappropriate comments. • Uses slang or inappropriate language.

Scoring Criteria for Persuasive Speeches, continued.

Scoring Criteria	Exceptional 5	Accomplished 4	Competent 3	Developing 2 / 1
Physical Expression Eye contact Posture Gesture Movement	• Strong eye contact with entire audience. • Posture is strong, commanding and purposeful. • Gestures and movement are natural and effective.	• Sustains eye contact with audience • Stands with purpose. • Uses some gestures and movement to enhance message. • Exhibits some nervous behavior.	• Eye contact is sporadic; speaker may look at only one part of audience or may use notes frequently. • Uses few gestures and limited and/or no movement. • Exhibits frequent and/or repetitive nervous behavior.	• Avoids eye contact; may read from motes or rarely glance at audience. • May slouch or stand off balance. • May be stiff. • Gestures/ movement are inappropriate, nervous, stiff, or nonexistent.
Vocal Expression Rate too fast/slow Volume too loud/soft Pitch too high/ low Articulation/pro- nunciation	• Speaker is enjoyable to hear, uses expression and emphasis. • Tone is conversational, but with purpose. • Voice sounds natural, neither patterned nor monotone. • Speaker pronounces words clearly and correctly.	• Speaker speaks clearly, using expression. • Conversational style is evident, but spontaneity may be lacking. • Speaker's pace and volume make speech easy to listen to and understand.	• Speaker may lack spontaneity and/or conversational style. A vocal pattern or monotone may be apparent. • Volume may be too soft or rate too fast.	• Speaker makes little attempt to use vocal techniques to communicate. • Displays a variety of weaknesses: monotone, soft volume, hesitation, verbal "fillers" (uh, um, y'know), giggling.
Persuasive Appeals Varied Creative Amplify the message	• Speaker integrates a variety of appeals. • Appeals are used creatively to amplify the message.	• Speaker uses required appeals. • Sometimes use does not strengthen persuasion.	• Speaker displays some objects, charts, graphs, etc., but relationship to content of speech may not be clear. • Quality may be inconsistent.	• Speaker uses insufficient aids or misuses aids. • Aids are of poor quality. • Aids do not enhance message.
Overall Impact Energy Enthusiasm Sincerity Originality/ creativity	• Speaker appears to have strong belief in proposition. • Speaker demonstrates desire to have the audience understand and agree. • Overall presentation is powerful and persuasive.	• Speaker appears to have some interest in topic. • Speaker is well prepared, displaying confident control of information. • Speaker makes clear attempt to communicate with audience.	• Speaker displays good preparation, but may lack confidence and enthusiasm. • Speaker speaks more to fulfill assignment than to communicate with audience.	• Speaker creates impression of being inadequately prepared. • Speaker lacks confidence and enthusiasm. Little attempt to communicate effectively with audience.

Persuasive Speech Evaluation Form

Speaker _____

The Speaking

How I saw you _____   **How I heard you** _____

Physical/Facial Expression   Vocal Expression

Eye Contact   Volume

Gestures/Movement

Evidence of Preparation

How You Prepared for the Experience   **Comments** _____

Introduction
- Grabs interest
- Thesis: Clearly states topic

Body
- Organization: Three major points of analysis and persuasion
- Use of Evidence: Three different source citations, only one from the Internet
- Use of Persuasive Language

Conclusion
- Clearly identifies what the speaker wants us to believe or do
- Has a logical, final ending, well rehearsed

Requirements Met _____   **Comments** _____
- Time: 5 minutes
- Outline: Intro, conclusion, three outlined points, bibliography
- Bibliography: 5 sources, only 1 electronic
- Professional appearance

Scoring Guide for Persuasive Speeches

Scoring Criteria	Exceptional 5	Accomplished 4	Competent 3	Developing 2 / 1
Introduction/Main				
Idea/conclusion attention getter opening				
Clear topic				
Well-supported identification of the problem				
Conclusion offers a final "call to action"				
Supporting Material				
Quoted material cited correctly				
Research material comes from a wide variety of sources				
Content/Language				
Speaker has considered audience				
Specific and well-chosen vocabulary				
Speech is free of fallacious reasoning				
Physical Expression				
Eye contact				
Posture				
Gesture				
Movement				
Vocal Expression				
Rate				
Volume				
Pitch				
Articulation/pronunciation				

Persuasive Audience Attitude Survey

Guidelines for Selecting a Topic
1. Avoid "faith."
2. Make sure the topic is controversial. Ask yourself: has the goal already been achieved? (The answer should be "no.")
3. Make sure the topic is practical. Ask yourself, is the goal possible to achieve? (The answer should be "yes.")
4. Make sure the topic is relevant: Ask yourself, can I make the audience care about this topic? (The answer should be "yes.")

Directions for Taking an Audience Survey
Part I
1. Carefully print one proposition at the top of each survey page. Make sure propositions are worded as complete sentences that call for a change in policy or practice.
2. Instruct *every* person in class to record their response in the appropriate column by printing their name and signing their initials. Double-check to make sure you have a response from every person in class.
3. If a person has a comment to make about the wording of the proposition or whether or not it meets the guidelines, have them write something in the comment section. Comments must be legible and must be signed.

Part II
1. Review the survey and comments.
2. Revise propositions as needed.
3. Rank your propositions from 1 (your top choice) to 3 (your last choice). Mark your ranks in the space provided.

Part III
1. Consider the information gathered in your survey as you construct your outline and be sure your strategies take into consideration the audience's reaction to your topic.
2. Turn in this survey with your final outline.

Name_____ Per_____

Proposition:_____

_____

_____

Strongly agree	Agree	Neutral	Disagree	Strongly disagree

Comments:

_____

Revised Proposition: _____

_____

_____

Rank _____

SECTION V
Listening

Listening skills are essential for effective communication and daily life. These listening activities were designed to encourage students to develop both active and critical listening skills. Active listening improves understanding and communication between the speaker and the audience. Critical listening enhances the listener's ability to evaluate messages.

Robbery Report

An activity that builds critical listening skills.

Materials
Robbery Report Worksheet

Procedure
1. Ask for three volunteers who think they are good listeners.
2. Tell the class that you will be playing the adult versions of "Telephone."
3. Explain that you will be reading a story called "Robbery Report" to one of the three volunteers while the other two wait outside.
4. After the two students leave the room, distribute copies of the Robbery Report Worksheet to the students in the audience.
5. Tell students their job is to jot down any changes or omissions each volunteer makes as he/she repeats the story.
6. Read the story to the volunteer in the room; use verbal and nonverbal communication skills when reading the story.
7. Ask the next volunteer to return to the classroom and have the first volunteer retell the report. Then ask the second volunteer to repeat it to the third volunteer.
8. With everyone present, read the original "Robbery Report."
9. Ask the three volunteers:
   • How did you feel as you tried to remember the message?
   • What made it difficult or easy to remember the message?
10. Ask the other students
   • How did the report change?
   • Was anything important left out?
   • What would have made it easier for the volunteers to remember the report?
   • What can get in the way of clear communication?

Teacher Tips
As a follow-up activity, you may want to ask three students to form a team and have one student tell his/her version of the story; then have another group member add things that were missed. When this person is finished, the third member adds any missing information.

Evaluation
The students' responses—either written or oral—to the questions in step 10 will indicate whether the activity was a success or not.

Robbery Report Worksheet

Robbery Report

Please listen carefully because I have to go to the hospital right away. I just called the police from the gas station on the corner. Wait here and report the robbery to them. I was walking into Johnson's Hardware Store, and this guy came running out and almost knocked me over. He was carrying a white bag, and it looked like he had a gun in his left hand. He was wearing a Levi jacket with the sleeves cut out and a green and blue plaid shirt and blue jeans with a hole in the right knee. He had skinny legs and a big stomach. He wore wire-rim glasses and high-top red Converse tennis shoes. He was bald and had a brown mustache and was six and a half feet tall, probably in his mid-thirties.

Directions: For each repetition of the report, note anything the person missed, added or changed from the previous report.

First Volunteer:

Second Volunteer:

Third Volunteer:

Good, Bad, and Ugly Listening

A strategy intended to build active listening skills.

Materials
Listening Rubric

Procedure
1. Select a student who is good-natured and a willing volunteer. Arrange two stools in front of the class and sit facing the student.
2. Ask the student to slowly recite the multiplication tables (the sevens work best) or something he or she knows by heart, such as the Pledge of Allegiance.
3. While the student is reciting, demonstrate good listening skills (e.g., sit attentively, make eye contact, etc.) for a short period of time; then segue into bad listening skills (e.g., slouch, avoid eye contact, etc.); then employ ugly listening skills (e.g., turn away form the speaker, start grading papers, eating, etc.).
4. At some point, the willing volunteer will either trip up, give up, or inquire "what are you doing???" When this happens, tell the class that it has just witnessed the effects of good, bad, and ugly listening.
5. Distribute Listening Rubric and discuss the three levels of listening in terms of the effects they had on the student speaker (e.g., "When you looked away, he lost his concentration and said 7 x 6 was 48.").
6. Let the students know that they will be assessed on their listening skills, using the rubric throughout different activities.

Teacher Tips
Possible activities for evaluating good, bad, and ugly listening:
- In groups of three, two students dialogue while the third student uses the Listening Rubric to evaluate his group members' listening skills. You may want to pre-assign students to behave "good, bad, or ugly, " allowing the evaluator a chance to observe the speaker's reactions to the variations in listening.
- After a student has finished a speech, randomly select another student to recount the speaker's main ideas and to compliment the speaker's best example.

Evaluation
1. You can use the rubric to assess students when they are asked to evaluate student speakers or presentations.
2. To attribute points for listening, students can be "given" 10 points for listening for the day, losing points only if they commit any of the bad or ugly violations on the rubric.

Listening Rubric

Listening	Good	Bad	Ugly
Nonverbal Feedback	• Sits attentively • Makes eye-contact with speaker • Takes notes if appropriate	• Slouches • Avoids eye-contact with speaker • Looks bored or busy with something else	• Turns or walks away from speaker • Engages in another activity • Makes distracting noises
Verbal Feedback	• Asks appropriate questions • Gives speaker a reply (e.g., "thank you.")	• Asks questions which are off topic or which have already been asked • Gives a flippant reply (e.g., "No, duh!")	• Talks while the speaker is speaking • May blurt out comments (e.g., "No way!")

Block Head

An activity intended to encourage good listening skills and following directions.

Materials

two identical sets of geometric children's blocks, or two identical sets of cardboard geometric shapes

Appendix 4: Barriers to Listening

Appendix 5: Ten Keys to Effective Listening

Block Head Evaluation Sheet

Procedure

1. Choose two students to sit back to back at desks at the front of the room.
2. Divide the blocks/shapes equally between the two students.
3. Allow the students to decide who will give the directions (the director) and who will receive them (the receiver).
4. The director builds his/her structure first from the pile of blocks.
5. Then proceed with one of the following options:
   - The director tells the receiver how to build the structure without any interaction; or
   - Allow the receiver to question the director as they progress (or as you watch their frustration levels rise).

Teacher Tips

1. You may want to begin the activity by distributing and discussing Appendix 4: Barriers to Listening and/or Appendix 5: Ten Keys to Effective Listening
2. Set time limits for the initial demonstration.
3. Instruct the rest of the class *not* to respond verbally or nonverbally ("sigh!") to the successes or failures of the participants.
4. Allow additional students to experience the activity. Be sure to build a new structure for each pair of students.
5. You'll discover that the students who go near the end of the day are better at following directions because they've learned the cues that work from observing the failed attempts of their predecessors.

Evaluation

Have students write a self-reflection, responding to the questions on the Block Head Evaluation Sheet.

Block Head Evaluation Sheet

Please respond candidly and specifically to the following questions:

1. What was the most frustrating portion of the exercise?

2. What was the most successful portion of the exercise?

3. What changes did you notice in the approach and/or language from the first group to the last group? (e.g., the difference between "a slanted block" and "a block with a 45° angle")

4. What conclusions can you draw about the nature of clear directions?

5. What conclusion can you draw about the nature of good listening regarding the following of directions?

Listen Up!

An exercise in using active listening and specific language to complete the Communication Model.

Materials
Appendix 4: Barriers to Listening and/or
Appendix 5: Ten Keys to Effective Listening

Procedure
The Communication Model is composed of the speaker, the message, the receiver, and the feedback.
1. You may want to begin the activity by distributing and discussing Appendix 4: Barriers to Listening and/or Appendix 5: Ten Keys to Effective Listening.
2. Ask two student volunteers to sit back to back at desks at the front of the room.
3. Hand one student (the artist) a piece of paper and pencil and the other (the director) a sheet of paper with an odd arrangement of shapes and lines of different sizes and line thickness.
4. Tell the director that he/she will be describing the picture under three different circumstances. Warn the director not to share the drawing with the artist or others who may be asked to observe. Tell the artist he is to draw whatever the director describes.

First time: The artist may not speak at all.

Second time: The students remain back to back, but the artist may ask questions.

Third time: The students sit face to face but do not share the picture yet. The director may use gestures and eye contact or question the artist—anything to get the job done. The artist can use any means available as well, short of actually looking at the drawing.

Evaluation
When the exercise is completed, ask the following questions of both the participants and observers:
- What did you learn about the communication process?
- What effect does eye contact have on communication?
- What effect does voice have on communication?
- What effect do gestures have on communication?
- What effect do questioning and clarification have on communication?

Active Listening Debate

A paraphrase activity that strengthens active listening skills.

Materials
flip chart
sticky dots
Active Listening Debate Evaluation Form

Procedure
1. Have the students brainstorm a list of topics suitable for debate. Do this on a flip chart or other permanent surface so it can be referred to as needed. These topics could be ones that they can discuss using only personal opinion, or you can have them do research.
2. Have the students vote on the top three topics. To do this, give each student two sticky dots. Ask the students to place a dot next to their top two issues or topics. They will debate the three topics that receive the most dots in order of student preference.
3. Ask the students to prepare a 2–3 minute presentation on the topic that was ranked first.
4. Discuss the criteria for evaluation on the Active Listening Debate Evaluation Form.
5. Set the rules for debate:
   • You need to actively listen to each student's speech. You may not take written notes.
   • You may not present your own arguments until you have repeated/summarized the arguments of the person who spoke directly before you.
   • The first person who speaks has the task of repeating the last speaker's arguments. This way he/she gets an opportunity to actively listen also.
   • If the speaker cannot summarize the person's arguments he/she may not speak.

Teacher Tips
1. You may pre-select who is going to speak in what order. That way, students know the person they have to listen to so that they can summarize the arguments.
2. You may allow the previous speaker to okay the summary given by the person who speaks. You also can ask the previous speaker to repeat any arguments missed so the speaker after him/her can summarize before speaking.

Evaluation
Complete the Active Listening Debate Evaluation Form.

Active Listening Debate Evaluation Form

Names: (Aff.)_____vs. (Neg.) _____

Speaker:_____

Topic:_____

	Knock Out	Won on Points	Draw	Sucker Punch	Comments
Summary	5	4	3	2 / 1	
Use of information	5	4	3	2 / 1	
Analysis	5	4	3	2 / 1	
Clash	5	4	3	2 / 1	
Etiquette	5	4	3	2 / 1	

Facts and Inferences

A useful exercise where students are required to read closely to find information.

Materials

Facts and Inference stories 1–3

Procedure

1. Read one of the Facts and Inference stories to students.
2. Give the students a listening test. Each test is a set of statements asking the students to determine: if the information was provided in the story (students would label the statement "T"); if the information contradicts what was presented in the story (students would label the statement "F"); or if the truth of the statement can't be determined on the basis of the story (students would label the statement "?").
3. Allow students 5 minutes to complete each test.

Teacher Tips

1. Copy the following pages after blocking out the answers written at the bottom. You may block out the written stories as well for more of a challenge.
2. You can vary the skill level required by allowing the students to look at the questions while the story is being read, allowing the students to read the story as you read it to them, or by adjusting the time allotted to finishing the test. You will need to adjust the instructions you give the students based on the actual situations you set up.
3. The test can be self-graded, students can grade each other's tests, or you can correct them.
4. Using several stories will provide a more challenging experience.
5. You can incorporate a cooperative element into the activity by allowing students to confer in teams to classify the statements in the test.
6. You can lead a debriefing discussion to help students understand why a response is correct.
7. You can use a reading from their class readings instead of those provided here.

Evaluation

1. You can base your evaluation on the scores students received on the listening tests.
2. You can evaluate student participation in debriefing discussions.
3. Give consideration to student scores that improve even as the stories become harder.

Facts and Inference Story 1

Instructions: In the story that I will read to you, you may assume that the whole story is accurate. I will give you a test after you have listened to the story. For each statement about the story put a "T" to indicate that the statement is definitely true, an "F" to indicate that the statement is definitely false, and "?" if you can't be certain on the basis of the story. If any part of the statement is doubtful, mark it "?"

John and Betty Smith are awakened in the middle of the night by a noise coming from the direction of their living room. Smith investigates and finds that the door opening into the garden, which he thought he had locked before going to bed, is standing wide open. Books and papers are scattered all over the floor around the desk in one corner of the room.

Statements about Story 1

_____ 1. Mrs. Smith was awakened in the middle of the night.

_____ 2. The door to the garden was open.

_____ 3. Smith locked the door from his living room to his garden before going to bed.

_____ 4. The books and papers were scattered between the time Mr. Smith went to bed and the time he was awakened.

_____ 5. Smith found that the door opening onto the garden was shut.

_____ 6. Mr. Smith did not lock the garden door.

_____ 7. John Smith was not awakened by a noise.

_____ 8. Nothing was missing from the room.

_____ 9. Mrs. Smith was sleeping when she and Mr. Smith were awakened.

_____ 10. While a burglar was the first thing Smith thought of when he was awakened, the story does not really make it clear that there was a burglar present.

_____ 11. The noise did not come from their garden.

_____ 12. There are papers scattered near the desk.

_____ 13. Mr. and Mrs. Smith were awakened in the middle of the night by a noise.

_____ 14. Smith saw no burglar in the living room.

Answers: 1.?, 2. T, 3. ?, 4. ?, 5. F, 6. ?, 7. F, 8. ?, 9. ?, 10. ?, 11. ?, 12. T, 13. ?, 14. ?

Facts and Inference Story 2

Instructions: In the story that I will read to you, you may assume that all of the story is accurate. I will give you a test after you have listened to the story. For each statement about the story put a "T" to indicate that the statement is definitely true, an "F" to indicate that the statement is definitely false, and "?" if you can't be certain on the basis of the story. If any part of the statement is doubtful, mark it "?"

A businessman had just turned out the lights in the store when a man appeared and demanded money. The owner opened a cash register. The contents of the cash register were scooped up, and the man sped away. A member of the police force was notified promptly.

Statements about Story 2

_____ 1. A man appeared after the owner had turned off his store lights.

_____ 2. The robber was a man.

_____ 3. The man did not demand money.

_____ 4. The man who opened the cash register was the owner.

_____ 5. The store owner scooped up the contents of the cash register and ran away.

_____ 6. Someone opened a cash register.

_____ 7. After the man who demanded the money scooped up the contents of the cash register, he ran away.

_____ 8. The cash register was left undisturbed.

_____ 9. While the cash register contained money, the story does not state how much.

_____ 10. The man demanding money held a gun to the businessman.

_____ 11. The robber demanded money of the owner.

_____ 12. A businessman turned out the lights.

_____ 13. The story concerns a series of events in which only three persons are referred to: The owner of the store; a man who demanded money; and a member of the police force.

_____ 14. The following events in the story are true: someone demanded money; a cash register was opened; its contents were scooped up; and a man dashed out of the store.

Answers: 1. ?, 2. ?, 3. F, 4. ?, 5. ?, 6. T, 7. ?, 8. F, 9. ?, 10. F, 11. ?, 12. T, 13. ?, 14. ?

Facts and Inference Story 3

Instructions: In the story that I will read to you, you may assume that all of the story is accurate. I will give you a test after you have listened to the story. For each statement about the story put a "T" to indicate that the statement is definitely true, an "F" to indicate that the statement is definitely false, and "?" if you can't be certain on the basis of the story. If any part of the statement is doubtful, mark it "?"

A man, his wife and sons, ages 11 and 14, drove across the country on a vacation trip in their three-year-old automobile. They started the trip on a Friday, the thirteenth day of the month. The wife said she did not like the idea of leaving on that day, and the man laughed at her statement. During the trip, the automobile radiator sprang a leak. The 14-year old boy nearly drowned. The 11-year-old boy became carsick for the first time in his life. The wife was badly sunburned. The man lost his fishing rod.

Statements about Story 3

_____ 1. There were fewer than two children in the family.

_____ 2. The sedan's radiator sprang a leak.

_____ 3. The wife really didn't mind leaving on Friday the thirteenth.

_____ 4. A fishing reel was lost.

_____ 5. The man turned back because his wife was superstitious.

_____ 6. The 11-year-old boy had never been carsick before.

_____ 7. The family's trip began on Friday the thirteenth.

_____ 8. The 11-year-old lost his fishing rod.

_____ 9. The 14-year-old boy fell into water.

_____ 10. The minivan was three years old.

_____ 11. The story mentions the name of the family taking the trip.

_____ 12. The wife spent too much time in the sun.

_____ 13. The make of the automobile in which the family made the trip was not mentioned in the story.

_____ 14. The man laughed at his wife's fears of Friday the thirteenth.

Answers: 1. F, 2. ?, 3. F, 4. ?, 5. F, 6. T, 7. T, 8. ?, 9. ?, 10. ?, 11. F, 12. T, 13. T, 14. ?

Sensory Overload

An activity intended to build good listening and the power of observation.

Materials

video equipment and video clip containing a large amount of action
Sensory Overload Evaluation Sheet

Procedure

1. Obtain a video clip containing a large amount of action (15-minute news clip, History Channel or Discovery Channel segment).
2. Show the clip with no explanation.
3. After the clip is over, tell the students they have 5 minutes to write a description of what they saw.
4. Ask each student to share his/her description with the class.
5. Discuss the validity of the students' observations.
6. Re-show the video to allow students to check their power of observation

Teacher Tips

1. Check with local news for longer clips.
2. Buy a prerecorded video: natural disaster—*World at War* or *Viet Nam: the 1000 Day War.*
3. Make sure you know what is in the clip. (It may help to outline it minute by minute.)
4. Use the following questions to prompt student discussion:
   - Who or what was involved?
   - What action took place?
   - What was said about the action?

Evaluation

Ask students to complete the Sensory Overload Evaluation Sheet.

Sensory Overload Evaluation Sheet

Please respond candidly and specifically to the following questions:

1. What did you observe and/or hear that others missed?

2. What did you miss that others observed and/or heard?

3. What did you do to ensure your observation was accurate?

4. What could you do to ensure you were more successful with your next observation?

SECTION VI
Multimedia

The explosion of media in form and volume makes analysis and production of multimedia a key element of many courses. These exercises will prepare the student to interpret and analyze a variety of multimedia presentations and to implement the appropriate, valid techniques in student-produced presentations.

Search Engine Comparison

An activity teaching students to research the search engine they most prefer.

Materials

Search Engine Comparison Evaluation Form

Procedure

1. Ask the students to read the Search Engines Quick Guide (http://www.infopeople.org/src/guide.html) and Search Tools Chart (http://www.infopeople.org/src/chart.html) to gain insight into how different search engines function.
2. Tell them to go on line and conduct a search on an educational issue such as project-based learning or another issue of your choice.
3. Tell them to experiment with using different search engines for the same topic, conducting the same search for each engine. Record the frequency and relevancy of the results.
4. Encourage them to experiment with advanced search options and links to other databases, if their chosen search engines contain these features.
5. Have the students complete the Search Engine Comparison Evaluation Form to compare their findings.

Search Engine Comparison Evaluation Form

Topic _____

	Search Engine 1 (name):	Search Engine 2 (name):	Search Engine 3 (name):	Search Engine 4 (name):
	_____	_____	_____	_____
Number of Hits				
Relevancy				
Speed				
Advanced Techniques				
Related Searching				

Bias Blasting

An activity that helps students evaluate Internet sources.

Materials
computer lab
Bias Blasting Worksheet
Tips for Searching the Web
Web Scavenger Hunt

Procedure
1. Take the students to a computer lab where all students may research their own topic at the same time.
2. Teach students how to find Internet sites using Tips for Searching the Web and Web Scavenger Hunt before beginning this activity.
3. Pass out the Bias Blasting Worksheet.
4. Give students a subject to research.
5. Instruct students to choose a Web site on their subject and complete the worksheet.

Teacher Tips
1. Reserve the computer lab to expedite the process of completing the assignment.
2. Have students use the Bias Blasting Worksheet to analyze all Internet sources they use in reports and presentations.

Evaluation
Grade the worksheet, examining its accuracy and thoroughness.

Bias Blasting Worksheet

1. Domain names (org, com, edu, gov, etc.) provide clues as to the source of the information. What is the domain name and what clues does it tell you about the source?

2. Search for information about the Web page authors. Does it tell why they are qualified to write this information? Can you contact them? Is there a reason to believe that they could have a strong opinion that they might be promoting?

3. When was the site last updated? Does it tell how current the information is?

4. Use the following questions to evaluate the **content** of the web page:
   What's the purpose of the page?

   Why was it created?

   Are there any awards, reputable directories, or guides? What are they?

   Are alternative viewpoints linked to or represented?

   Is the page a spoof or parody of another page?

5. Is there a bibliography (list of resources)? If some of the resources look questionable, check on them. Click on the Web links. Try to verify book information at sources like Amazon.com (http://www.amazon.com).

6. Choose one of the reliable Internet sources you navigated today. Create a bibliography entry for that site using the information provided on one of the helpful links.

Tips for Searching the Web

Search Strategy
- Regardless of the search tool you use, developing an effective search strategy is essential if you hope to obtain satisfactory results. A simplified, generic search strategy might consist of the following steps:
- Formulate the research question and its scope.
- Identify the important concepts within the question.
- Identify search terms to describe those concepts.
- Consider synonyms and variations of those concepts.
- Prepare your search logic.

How
- Click on the search button.
- If you know the address to the site, type it in.
- You may also type in the URL of the search engine.

Basic Operators for a Search
- Use a + (plus) sign to require a keyword. For example, this will search for pages that contain both the words "hotel" and "Florida." Hotel + Florida.
- Use a – (minus) sign to exclude a keyword. For example, this will search for pages that contain the wording "marketing" but do not contain the word "sales." Marketing – sales.
- Use " " (quotation marks) to find an exact phrase. For example, this will search for pages that have the words "Phantom Menace" appearing together. "Phantom Menace."
- Use an * (asterisk) as a wild card to search for multiple forms of the word. For example, the following search will search for big, bigger, biggest: big*.

Web Scavenger Hunt

Name_____

Directions

Conduct a keyword search or use a directory to answer the questions below. Include the URL in your answer. Click the search feature on your browser, or type in the URL of a search engine:

Alta Vista http://www.altavista.com/   **Webcrawler** http://www.webcrawler.com/

Search http://www.search.com/   **Yahoo** http://www.yahoo.com/

Name five criminals who are on the FBI's Ten Most Wanted list. _____

URL_____

What is the population of the world? _____

What is the population of the United States? _____

URL_____

A live cam is a particular camera that is always turned on and the display can be accessed via the Internet. Find a live cam shot of a famous landmark. Include the URL.

Landmark _____

URL_____

Find a recipe for masala dosa.

List the ingredients._____

What country does this come from? _____

URL_____

Find a sound that can be made by a mammal or a bird.

Sound _____

URL_____

Refining a Search

Finding specific information on the Internet can be very challenging. The Internet contains an enormous number of sites and information on every topic imaginable. To find information more easily, there are many advanced searching techniques you can try.

For example:

Using + before a keyword requires that the word be found in all the search results.

Using – before a keyword excludes web sites containing that keyword.

Using quotation marks around a set of words narrows the search results to sites containing those words in that exact sequence only.

Directions

Using AltaVista, http://www.altavista.com try the following. Conduct a search on Beanie Babies. Indicate the number of hits you receive with each of the following search parameters.

Beanie Baby _____   "Beanie Baby" _____

Beanie – Baby _____   title: "Beanie Baby" _____

Beanie + Baby _____   url: "Beanie Baby" _____

Try the same experiment using the keywords "consumer reports."

Consumer reports _____   "consumer reports" _____

Consumer – reports _____   title: "consumer reports" _____

Consumer + reports _____   url: "consumer reports" _____

The Pathos, Ethos, and Logos of *Other People's Money*

An exercise in classical analysis.

Materials
equipment and video of *Other People's Money*
Three Classical Elements of Persuasion
Evaluating a Speaker With Classical Elements of Persuasion

Procedure
1. Use Three Classical Elements of Persuasion to give an overview of ethos, pathos, and logos
2. Ask students which of the three elements appeals to them when someone is trying to persuade them.
3. Cue up the film *Other People's Money* to the scene featuring Gregory Peck and Danny DeVito giving back-to-back speeches. Students do not have to be familiar with the film; they need only to know that both speakers are trying to persuade an audience to buy their ideas.
4. After Gregory Peck is finished with his speech, pause the film to discuss which specific elements of persuasion he employed.
5. Resume the film. When Danny DeVito is finished with his speech, stop the movie and ask the students to analyze his performance in light of the three elements of persuasion.
6. Ask the students which speaker they found to be the most persuasive and why? You also may want students to consider whether the order of the speakers influenced their persuasive impact. (If two classes have the assignment, you may want to show the second class the speeches in reverse order and debrief on the effects.)

Teacher Tips
1. You may want to run this activity as a group discussion.
2. You may ask students to complete Evaluating a Speaker With Classical Elements of Persuasion.
3. You may want to discuss the validity or reliability of the elements of persuasion *or* the validity of inductive *vs.* deductive reasoning.
4. For homework, you could ask students to analyze a TV courtroom drama or another scene from a movie or play, such as the speeches of Brutus and Antony from *Julius Caesar*. Here's an abbreviated list of some of the titles that have worked in the past: *Erin Brockovich, A Time to Kill, Good Will Hunting, Wall Street, Mrs. Doubtfire,* and *Office Space.*

Evaluation
Whether written or oral, student responses should be specific—referring to terminology, e.g., parallelism, tone, etc.

Three Classical Elements of Persuasion

Ethos
Ethical Appeal: The credibility of the speaker, writer, or source

Pathos
Emotional Appeal as conveyed through:

The language of the speaker
- diction
- syntax
- connotative words
- repetition
- parallelism
- analogies

The appearance of the speaker
- dress, hair, etc.
- movement
- tone of voice

The emotional state of the audience
- prejudices
- occasion

Logos
Logical Appeal:

Inductive reasoning—specific to general evidence/assertion/conclusion

Example:

Evidence:	• Org ate the red plant and died that night.
	• Ugh ate the red plant and died that night.
	• Ick ate the red plant and died that night.
Assertion:	The red plant killed them.
Conclusion:	The red plant is deadly.

Deductive reasoning—general to specific major premise/minor premise/conclusion

Sample syllogism:

Major premise	The red plant is deadly.
Minor premise	Ur ate the red plant.
Conclusion	Ur will die.

Evaluating a Speaker With Classical Elements of Persuasion

Speaker #1_____

   1. Comment on his/her **ethos**:

      How credible did you think he/she was and why?

   2. Comment on the **pathos** of the speaker:

      How did his/her appearance influence you?

      How did his/her tone of voice and bodily movement affect you?

   3. Comment on the speaker's use of language (consider diction, syntax, connotative words, repetition, parallelism, analogies):

      How did the emotional state of the audience affect the speaker's message?

   4. Comment on the **logos** of the speaker:

      Did he/she primarily use inductive or deductive reasoning? Give examples.

   5. Overall, would you say that the speaker's performance was dominated by **ethos**, **pathos**, or **logos**?

Speaker #2_____

1. Comment on his/her **ethos**:

   How credible did you think he/she was and why?

2. Comment on the **pathos** of the speaker:

   How did his/her appearance influence you?

   How did his/her tone of voice and bodily movement affect you?

3. Comment on the speaker's use of language (consider diction, syntax, connotative words, repetition, parallelism, analogies):

   How did the emotional state of the audience affect the speaker's message?

4. Comment on the **logos** of the speaker:

   Did he/she primarily use inductive or deductive reasoning? Give examples.

5. Overall, would you say that the speaker's performance was dominated by **ethos**, **pathos**, or **logos**?

_____

Which of the preceding speakers did you find most persuasive? Why?

Do you think that the order in which they spoke had any bearing on their persuasive impact? Explain.

Fun With Fallacies

An exercise in logical analysis.

Materials

Three Classical Elements of Persuasion (page 15)
Fallacies: Errors in Logic
Listening for Faulty Reasoning/Logical Fallacies (page 21)
Fun with Fallacies Evaluation Form

Procedure

1. Use Three Classical Elements of Persuasion to review ethos, pathos, and logos.
2. Give an overview of logical fallacies using Fallacies: Errors in Logic, or for the more advanced class, complete list of fallacies appearing in Listening for Faulty Reasoning/Logical Fallacies.
3. Ask the students to do the following:
   a. Clip a full-page ad from a magazine.
   b. Mount the ad on a piece of poster board or construction paper.
   c. Write an analysis of the ad using the three elements of persuasion and tape it to the back of the poster.
   d. In big bold letters, proclaim the dominant fallacy in the ad on the front of the poster.
   e. Reduce the ad to a three-line syllogism and print that in big bold letters on the front of the poster.
   f. Be prepared to explain the analysis to the class.

Teacher Tips

You may want to limit the content of the ads to exclude alcohol and cigarettes.

Evaluation

Use the Fun with Fallacies Evaluation Form to assess the students.

Fallacies: Errors in Logic

List of the (un)Lucky Seven

1. **Sweeper** (sweeping generalization/over-simplification)
   Eating all red food is dangerous!

2. **Beggar** (begging the question)
   Eating red plants is dangerous because they're unsafe to eat.

3. **Spinner** (circular logic)
   Eating red plants is dangerous. You shouldn't eat red plants. Therefore, they're not safe!

4. **False Analogy**
   Red plants prey on humans like deadly serpents; we destroy deadly serpents; therefore, red plants must be destroyed !

5. **Ad Hominem** (against the man)
   Org is dumb. If Org eats red plants, I won't eat red plants.
   or
   Ugh is smart. If Ugh eats red plants, I'll eat red plants.

6. **Post hoc ergo propter hoc** (if this, then this . . .)
   If I don't eat the red plant, I'll live forever!

7. **Non sequitur** (leapin' logic!)
   Red plants are deadly; therefore, you should eat toads!

Fun With Fallacies Evaluation Form

	Shall We Call You Aristotle?	Impeccable	Good	Flawed	Oops?	Comments
Art	5	4	3	2	1	
Analysis	5	4	3	2	1	
Proclamation	5	4	3	2	1	
Syllogism	5	4	3	2	1	

Making "Movie Day" Matter

An activity you can use in any class where students watch a movie.

Materials
movie or tape of TV show relevant to curriculum
Movie or TV Show Review Worksheet
Appendix 6: Video Terms
Movie or TV Show Review Worksheet

Procedure
1. Select a movie or tape of a TV show that has relevance to the curriculum.
2. Ask the students to take notes while watching the film.
3. After seeing the movie, give each student a copy of the Movie or TV Show Review Worksheet.
4. Ask the students, individually or in groups, to write an essay that develops the questions in the handout.

Teacher Tips
1. Discuss the terms in the handout before showing the movie.
2. Do not give the students the handout until after seeing the movie, or they might write only a few notes and not develop an essay.
3. You may want to distribute Appendix 6: Video Terms so students can use the terminology when discussing and writing about the film.

Evaluation
You can evaluate students on the specificity of their responses to the questions on the Movie or TV Show Review Worksheet

Movie or TV Show Review Worksheet

What scenes most strongly express the theme?

Plot: Is the plot interesting? Is it believable? Is it too complicated? Are there sub-plots? What influences the characters in their actions?

Script: Does the characters' dialogue seem real? Has the script developed sufficient motivation for the characters' actions? Are there unnecessary digressions and irrelevancies?

Acting: Did the characters seem real? Did the portrayal of the characters cause you to become emotionally involved in the film? Give examples.

Setting, costumes, make-up: Did the settings, costumes, and make-up create the right atmosphere? Were the costumes expressive of various personalities? Were settings, costumes, and make-up appropriate for the era depicted?

Sound Effects: What kinds of sound effects were used? Did the sounds add or detract from the film? Did they make the film seem more real? Were they effective? Explain.

Musical Effects: Did the music set the correct mood for the show? Did the music flow smoothly from one theme to another?

Photography: Did the lighting, composition, camera placement, and camera movements help to develop the plot and theme? How? What images seemed most effective? Did the photography cause the viewer to become involved in the action? How so?

In the Blink of an Eye

An exercise to help students understand psychological closure.

Materials

video recording equipment
In the Blink of an Eye Scoring Guide
In the Blink of an Eye Peer Feedback Form

Procedures

1. Discuss the concept of psychological closure—when basic actions are left out, the brain fills them in based on previous experience.
2. Review the issues and elements involved in making a short video that depicts a character en route to a destination (e.g., a student is going to the office to get a pass and will return to the classroom).
   a. How long will the film be, if it is filmed in its entirety?
   b. What essential portions could be filmed to make the video more interesting?
   c. What essential shots must be made to get the idea across?
   d. What will the brain accept and fill in for the audience? How might the audience be sent inadvertently in the wrong direction?
3. Divide the class into groups and have each appoint a director who will explain the group's goals to the class.
4. Ask the groups to write a short scene they wish to film. (See Teacher Tip 3.)
5. You *must* evaluate these ideas prior to filming. This will eliminate any scenes that may be dangerous to the students or deal with inappropriate subject matter.
6. Return the evaluations and have each group film their scene, using as little action as possible.
7. Distribute In the Blink of an Eye Peer Feedback Form and ask one group to share the video with the rest of the class (the audience). The group is not to introduce or explain what it is trying to do.
8. Ask the audience to complete Part 1 of Peer Feedback.
9. Have the group's director explain the goal of the video.
10. Ask the audience to complete the second part of Peer Feedback.
11. Have the group retape its video using the Peer Feedback sheets as guides, providing the least information necessary to convey its idea.
12. Ask the group to consider the effect that audio could have on the mood/tone of its video.
13. Have the group choose two separate audio tracks that would alter the video and audio-dub the scene twice.
14. Ask the group to re-present the video and tell the audience to complete the final portion of Peer Feedback.
15. Repeat the procedure with the other groups.

Teacher Tips

1. Be prepared to give direct instruction on all elements of developing a video.
2. Be prepared to lead a group discussion on the effect of music and sound on film production.
3. You must approve the scene ideas before taping begins. This will eliminate any scenes that may be dangerous to the students or deal with inappropriate subject matter.

Evaluation

1. You may use the In the Blink of an Eye Scoring Guide.
2. Students may evaluate each other using the In the Blink of an Eye Peer Feedback Form.

In the Blink of an Eye Peer Feedback Form

Film name:_____ Critic:_____
Videographers:

_____

_____

_____

_____

Part 1: After the first filming

1. Was this video difficult to watch? Why/Why not?

2. What was the action the videographers were trying to present?

3. List the leaps your mind was expected to make in this video.

4. What essential scenes were included to present this idea?

Part 2: After Hearing the Director

1. What extraneous scenes could have been omitted in this video?

2. Which elements mislead the audience?

Part 3: After the Addition of Audio Track

1. What effect did the first music/sound track have on the video?

2. What effect did the second music/sound track have on the video?

In the Blink of an Eye Scoring Guide

	Hitchcock would be proud!	Excellent	Good	Fair	Oops!
Appropriate length/subject matter	5	4	3	2	I
Interest level	5	4	3	2	I
Meaningful essential shots	5	4	3	2	I
Clear hints given to replace missing scenes	5	4	3	2	I

Comments:

The Movie Trailer

An exercise in enticement.

Materials

video camera for each group of students
movie trailers demonstrating different techniques and content
Storyboard
Rubric for Movie Trailer
Appendix 6: Video Terms

Procedure

1. Play the trailer examples for the class and discuss the various techniques used. You may wish to distribute copies of Appendix 6: Video Terms to help the students understand the process.
2. Divide the class into groups and tell them they will be making a 45 second to 1.5 minute movie trailer based on a topic of your choice.
3. Ask each group to create a storyboard, using the form below, and submit it to you for approval.
4. Once you have approved the storyboards, tell the students they may make their trailer.
5. Before they begin, review the criteria for judging the video: sequence, dialogue, setting.
6. Schedule the video screenings.

Teacher Tips

1. You can have the students base their trailers on books or issues studied in the class.
2. Make sure the focus doesn't become a summary but instead creates a wonder about the subject.

Evaluation

1. Evaluate the students' storyboard worksheets.
2. Use the Rubric for Movie Trailer to judge the video.

Storyboard

Title:_____ Producer: _____

Date:_____ Page ____ of ____

1. Video	2. Video	3. Video
Audio	Audio	Audio

1. Video	2. Video	3. Video
Audio	Audio	Audio

Rubric for Movie Trailer

Name: _____

	Good	OK	Unacceptable
Sequence	3	2	I
Dialogue	3	2	I
Setting	3	2	I

Comments:

Selling the Product

An exercise in commercial persuasion.

Materials

Commercial Formats
Storyboard (page 177)
Program Planning Guide
Rubric for Commercials
video taping equipment (optional)

Procedure

1. Use Commercial Formats to give an overview of the most commonly used formats for television commercials
2. Ask students to give examples of each of the formats that they have viewed on television.
3. If available, show video clips of each type of commercial.
4. Divide the students into groups and ask them to write a storyboard using one of the commercial formats. You could assign the format or allow students to choose their own.
5. Have each group fill out the Program Planning Guide. After you approve the storyboards and planning guides, have the groups produce their commercials.
6. Depending on supplies and time, groups could produce and present their commercials either on video tape or in front of the class.

Teacher Tips

1. Carefully check the storyboard for possible innuendoes and any actions that may be dangerous or violate school rules.
2. Do not allow students to copy an existing commercial.
3. You may want the students to create their own products and assign an original name, price, description of the container, and availability of the product.
4. Encourage the students to include themselves in the commercial to enhance its believability.
5. Encourage students to use a variety of shots.
6. Remind students that audio is also very important: The audience must be able to hear the dialogue.

Evaluation

Complete the Rubric for Commercials.

Commercial Formats

Demonstration: The feature or benefit of the product is demonstrated rather than explained.

Musical: May use a song or jingle.

Narrative: Creates a situation that is highly personal, deeply moving and emotionally strong. Does not always concentrate exclusively on the product.

Problem-Solution: This format deals with a specific consumer problem. The product feature represents the solution that is a specific consumer benefit.

Product Alone: Shows the product by itself or represented symbolically.

Slice of Life: Development of a plot with a beginning, middle, and end in which there is a discovery about the product or people who make it.

Spokesman: The announcer speaks directly to viewers about the product.

Testimonial: Given by people who have used and liked the product.

Program Planning Guide

Group Members:_____ Shooting Date: _____

1. What shots will you be shooting? (Describe these.)

2. Location of shooting:

3. Who will be needed for the shooting? (List crew and talent; classes they're from.)

4. What props will be necessary for shooting? (Be sure to talk to talent about clothing.)

5. What equipment will be needed? (Extension cords?)

6. Will any special arrangements need to be made? Have you made these arrangements?
   (Please list individuals you contacted for usage purposes.)

7. Are there any shooting problems that might require teacher assistance?

8. Estimated time needed for shooting and returning to class:

9. Equipment inventory?

   Camera:

   Tripod:

   Light and light stand:

   Special materials:

Rubric for Commercials

Names: _____

_____

_____

_____

_____

_____

	Good	OK	Unacceptable
Originality/ Creativity	3	2	1
Adherence to Format	3	2	1
Storyline/ Content	3	2	1
Video Techniques	3	2	1

Comments:

Commercial in a Bag

An exercise in analysis.

Materials

unidentifiable household objects or gadgets

paper bags

Information Sheet for Commercial in a Bag

Storyboard (page 177)

Rubric for Commercials (page 182)

video taping equipment (optional)

Procedure

Day One

1. Fill paper bags with unusual household objects or gadgets that are hard to identify. There should be one object in each bag.
2. Divide the students into groups and let each group choose a paper bag.
3. Tell students that each bag contains a product for which they must write a commercial.
4. After students open their bags, allow them time to respond to questions on the Information Sheet for Commercial in a Bag.
5. Next, ask the students to develop a storyboard for their commercial.
6. Explain the criteria on which the commercials will be judged using the Rubric for Commercials.

Day Two (optional)

Have students film their commercials.

Teacher Tips

1. Make a few extra product bags, since some will go missing or break by the end of the day.
2. Don't let students choose a second bag. They'll want to "shop" for their item, and this creates chaos!

Evaluation

1. Use the Rubric for Commercials to assess the commercials on the students' ability to be creative and to look beyond what the product was originally intended for.
2. Commercials must be rated G in order to receive a grade.
3. Ask the students to analyze each other's commercials using the three elements of persuasion. Alternately, ask them to identify fallacies.

Information Sheet for Commercial in a Bag

Group Names: _____

_____

_____

_____

_____

In preparing your **G-Rated** commercial, your group must first analyze your product by answering the following questions. When you are finished, storyboard your commercials, and then staple this sheet to your storyboard.

1. What item are you selling?

2. What is the name of your product?

3. How much does it cost?

4. Where can a consumer buy it? Is it available in stores (what kind) or do I have to order it?

5. What are the reasons I should buy it?

6. Why is it better than other brands?

7. Create a jingle or slogan for your product.

The Green Light Project

Making a pitch that has a purpose.

Materials

The Green Light Project Assignment Sheet
Program Planning Guide (page 181)
Rubric for Commercials (page 182)

Procedure

1. Distribute and review The Green Light Project Assignment Sheet.
2. Have the class discuss projects that would help the school/class.
3. Ask each student to write his/her proposal.
4. After you have evaluated the papers, ask each student to orally present the treatment to the entire class.
5. Encourage class members to give suggestions.
6. Ask each student to revise his/her proposal in light of the class comments and fill out a Program Planning Guide.

Teacher Tips

1. Have a list of possible projects to share with the class if students cannot think of topics.
2. Monitor comments from the students as they listen to the oral presentations to make sure they are constructive.

Evaluation

1. Evaluate the written proposals and the Program Planning Guides.
2. You may use the Rubric for Commercials to evaluate the oral presentations.

The Green Light Project Assignment Sheet

Imagine that one of the major networks is offering a grant of $50,000 to high school students to produce an hour-long show. To be given a "green light" for the grant, you must present a treatment or overview of what you plan to produce if you are awarded the money. Include the following in your proposal:

- What is the object or purpose of your show? What are you trying to accomplish? Do you want to entertain, persuade, or inform?

- What method will you use? Will you use a documentary or news format?

- Will your production be a sitcom or drama?

- Outline your storyline.

- Where will it be shot? How many people will be involved? Will you use music?

- What arrangements will have to be made? How will you accomplish this? Whom will you have to call or contact?

After you have written the proposal:

- Turn it in to your teacher.

- "Pitch" your proposal orally to the class. Be prepared to respond to their comments/suggestions.

- Rewrite the proposal, including suggestions and/or giving reasons why you did not accept certain suggestions.

- Fill out a Program Planning Guide.

Enlightening Presentations with PowerPoint

An opportunity to develop communication skills through PowerPoint presentations.

Materials
computer lab
Enlightening Presentations with PowerPoint Assignment Sheet
PowerPoint Presentation Evaluation Sheet
video taping equipment (optional)

Procedure
1. Reserve computer lab.
2. Teach students basic PowerPoint skills.
3. Pass out and review the assignment sheet below.
4. Teach the terms and/or concept area necessary for analysis.
5. Divide subject areas and assign projects.
6. Distribute the PowerPoint Presentation Evaluation Sheet and discuss the criteria for assessment before you begin.
7. Schedule the presentations.

Teacher Tips
1. Using the assignment in groups of two or three may reduce presentation time and student stress.
2. Reserve the computer lab to expedite the process of completing the assignment.
3. Have students turn in the PowerPoint presentations on disk or CD to save as future models.
4. Videotape presentations to serve as models for future presentation.
5. Students may enjoy discussing the effect the PowerPoint presentations had on convincing them to read a book or learn a new concept.

Evaluation
Use the PowerPoint Presentation Evaluation Sheet and the presentations to assess each student or group.

Enlightening Presentations
with PowerPoint Assignment Sheet

For a Presentation on a Book

Choose a book you've read this semester and make a PowerPoint presentation that includes the following:

Slide 1   Book title and author. Your name and period number.

Slide 2   Describe the setting (place and time).

Slide 3   Describe the main characters (no more than three).

Slide 4   Briefly summarize what situation the character(s) find themselves in.

Slide 5   Note the genre of the book (love story, horror, thriller, biography, etc.). Describe the writer's style (simple, complex, childlike, filled with imagery, funny, dark, realistic, fairytale-like, etc.); include one representative sentence from the book that typifies the writer's style.

Slide 6   Give the book a commendation and recommendation. What did the writer do well? What shortcomings does the book have, and how could the book be improved?

Slide 7   List one or two of the themes of the book. Remember that theme is not topic. A topic becomes a theme when you develop it with an opinion or point of view, i.e., love is a topic, not a theme, but "love is fleeting" is a theme.

Slide 8–?   Answer the following questions that apply. Use as many slides as you need. Are the characters real? Is the situation real? Can you relate to the situation? How does point of view influence the plot? How does setting affect the plot? Was there an extraneous scene? Or a scene that should have been added for clarity? What type of reader would enjoy this book?

Assignment Requirements

Time: Presentations longer than 10 minutes will be penalized.

Each slide must include one or two representative visual elements. Graphics can be a work of art, a photo, or even something you've created on your own.

PowerPoint vs. *Power paragraph:* You are limited to no more than fifteen words on any one slide. Be brief and to the point. Use bullets if that helps organize and clarify.
Sound is optional, but impressive.

For a Presentation on a Concept

Choose a concept you've read this semester and make a PowerPoint presentation that includes the following:

Slide 1   Your name and period number. Name of the concept.

Slide 2   Describe the concept.

Slide 3   Describe the concept's uses or applications. (Note: a separate slide may be used for each application or use.)

Slide 4   Briefly illustrate a specific situation the concept could be used in.

Slide 5   Investigate when the concept originated.

Slide 6   Investigate who originated the concept.

Slide 7   Investigate where the concept originated.

Slide 8   Investigate how/why the concept spread.

Slide 9   Rate the concept's usefulness today.

Slide 10   Rate the concept's future impact.

Assignment Requirements

Time: Presentations longer than 10 minutes will be penalized.

Each slide must include one or two representative visual elements. Graphics can be a work of art, a photo, or even something you've created on your own.

PowerPoint vs. *Power paragraph:* You are limited to no more than fifteen words on any one slide. Be brief and to the point. Use bullets if that helps organize and clarify.
Sound is optional, but impressive.

PowerPoint Presentation Evaluation Sheet

Scoring Criteria	Exceptional	Accomplished	Competent	Developing

Organization/ Content
  Complete
  Interesting
  Appropriate
  Clear
	5	4	3	2 / 1

PowerPoint Slides
  Creative
  Graphic/Art
  Relevant
  Complete
  Word limit
  Easy to see/hear
	5	4	3	2 / 1

Delivery
  Eye contact
  Gestures
  Vocal control
  Vocal variety
  Posture
  Effective han-dling
	5	4	3	2 / 1

Overall
  Time guidelines
  Preparation
  Practice
	5	4	3	2 / 1

Point of View: Changing Perspectives

An exercise in perspective through dialogue.

Materials

Dinner for One
Point of View Evaluation Sheet

Procedure

1. Lecture and model point of view. Discuss how it changes as the environment changes, as the person who is speaking or writing changes, and as the topic changes. You can use movie clips, short stories, novels, debate/trial transcripts, etc. to illustrate point of view.
2. Explain the elements used to show changed perspective: objective (what the speaker wants), problem (the behavior of the other speaker), and action (what the speaker says/does in reaction).
3. Give the students Dinner for One. Ask them to interpret the scene based on different situations. The dialogue will not change, but the emotions and actions will change with each set of circumstances. Have them practice and perform the scenes.
4. Divide the students into pairs or small groups and have them create their own dialogue. Students should strive to have at least three different perspectives in their material.
5. Distribute the Point of View Evaluation Sheet and discuss the criteria for assessment.
6. Ask the pairs or groups to exchange their scenes so that another group will perform what the original group created.

Teacher Tips

1. Students will need to write the situations first and then create the dialogue. They can revise the situation if needed.
2. Students need to include a range of emotions in their situations.
3. The dialogue needs to remain neutral so that interpretations can reveal different emotions.
4. You can use any topics or situations.

Evaluation

Use the Point of View Evaluation Sheet to assess the student groups.

Dinner for One
Background

Situation One
The circumstances

Two people are out on a third date. They are in a restaurant having a late dinner. They are having a pleasant conversation until someone mentions the word "relationship."

Avery's Objective and Problem

Avery is getting older and realizes that he would like a family and a stable home life. Objective: In an effort to overcome my insecurities and lack of confidence, I would like Paige to make an early commitment to establish a lasting relationship. Initially he has some confidence as she responds nicely, then this confidence begins to wane as he realizes that she is not giving honest responses, and finally he becomes anxious and loses all confidence as he concludes that she is totally insincere and not interested in him.

Paige's Objective and Problem

Paige is not ready to settle down. This is only the first date and she feels that Avery is moving too fast. Objective: In an effort to conceal my apprehension regarding commitment I try to maintain a light façade. Her actions reflect her desire to remain uncommitted. As the conversation continues, she gets nervous and standoffish.

Situation Two
The circumstances

Two people have been friends for a long time. They are in a restaurant having a late dinner. They are having a pleasant conversation until Avery mentions that he wants to change the relationship.

Avery's Objective and Problem

Avery has come to realize that his feelings have grown beyond friendship for Paige. Objective: I want to find a means of expressing my inner feelings for Paige. He is concerned with what Paige's reaction is. He moves from excited about the prospect of a new relationship to one of resolute acceptance of the old one.

Paige's Objective and Problem

Paige does not want to change the relationship. Objective: I want to ensure that Avery's feelings are not hurt, and I want to remain as friends. Paige is sincere but not brutally honest with him.

Situation Three

The circumstances

Two people have been married for fifteen years. They have had a trial separation and are having dinner to discuss the relationship.

Avery's Objective and Problem

Avery wants to rekindle the relationship and get back together. Objective: I want to reestablish my loving relationship with my wife. He moves from being elated and hopeful about reconciliation with Paige to anger over her rejection.

Paige's Objective and Problem

Paige has come to tell Avery she wants a divorce. Objective: I want to end my relationship with my husband. She is cool, calm and collected. She has to remain emotionally unattached so that she can squash any attempt at rekindling the romance by Avery.

Dialogue

Scene: An intimate table in an upscale restaurant.

Avery	I'm glad that you could make it this evening.
Paige	I'm sorry I'm late.
Avery	That's OK. I understand.
Paige	Have you ordered?
Avery	No, I wasn't sure what you would like this evening.
Paige	Could I see the menu?

(Pause)

Avery	Where is this relationship going?
Paige	Relationship? Is this a relationship?
Avery	Yes, I think we need to define where we are headed.
Paige	Is this headed somewhere?
Avery	I thought we were compatible.
Paige	Not like that.
Avery	Does this mean we don't have a future together?
Paige	A future with you was not what I had in mind.
Avery	I don't understand, why?
Paige	I don't think you could ever meet my emotional needs.
Avery	You haven't given me the chance.
Paige	Yes I did, you just misunderstood.
Avery	I see no point in continuing this any further.

Point of View Evaluation Sheet

Evaluation of Original Written Situations

	Screen Writers' Guild!	Excellent	Good	Fair	Oops
Neutral Dialogue	5	4	3	2	I
Three Different Circumstances (with a range of emotions)	5	4	3	2	I
Dialogue Objectives (clear purpose to the dialogue)	5	4	3	2	I

Evaluation of Spoken Scene

Dialogue Partners:_____ and _____

	An Oscar awaits you!	Your interpretation of the words and emotions is very good.	You are doing well with the words but the emotion is lacking.	You have more work to do.	Ben Stein is more expressive.
Expression:					
• Body Language	5	4	3	2	I
• Facial Expressions	5	4	3	2	I
• Clarity	5	4	3	2	I
• Volume	5	4	3	2	I
• Pace	5	4	3	2	I
• Tone	5	4	3	2	I
Actions/Reactions	5	4	3	2	I
Goal of Dialogue Achieved	5	4	3	2	I

SECTION VII
Oral Interpretation

Oral interpretation is the reading and interpretation of literature through the use of voice and body. It helps with the understanding of literary works across the curriculum. Activities can range from reading aloud to close analysis of a text. Interpretation requires the participant to follow as closely as possible the intent of the author.

Say It Right!

A cross-curricular reading exercise that emphasizes pronunciation.

Materials

copies of a selected text
Say It Right! Evaluation Form

Procedure

1. Choose a passage (six to ten lines) from a text or selected reading for the oral presentation and prepare copies of the material for the class.
2. Announce that the class will be giving oral presentations of the selected text and distribute the copies.
3. Review the text.
4. Distribute the Say It Right! Evaluation Form and go over the criteria for assessment.
5. Give students 10 minutes to prepare their readings. Students may want to:
   - consult you or a dictionary for proper pronunciation
   - mark the passage with a pencil to indicate pauses or words to emphasize
   - practice with another student
   - practice some more!
6. Have students read aloud their passages and discuss the presentations.

Teacher Tips

You may want to ask the class to assess each presentation.

Evaluation

Use the Say It Right! Evaluation Form to grade the presentations.

Say It Right! Evaluation Form

Name_____ Period _____

Oral reading of _____

	Got it!	Almost	What?
Pronunciation (Saying the words right)	3	2	I
Enunciation (Saying the words clearly)	3	2	I
Inflection (Emphasizing the right words)	3	2	I
Rate (Pausing in the right places)	3	2	I

Comments:

Duolog

An exercise in writing and delivering effective dialogue to give better understanding to literary characters or historical figures.

Materials

Your Basic Quaddie
Duolog Evaluation Form
Appendix 7: Warm Up Exercises (optional)

Procedure

1. Divide the class into pairs and distribute Your Basic Quaddie to explain a *duolog*.

2. Ask each pair to write a duolog. The duolog should contain at least two pages of dialogue between two people: two literary characters, two historical figures, etc.

3. Explain the specific requirements of the duolog:
   * all information about names, setting, and action must come from the dialogue
   * the dialogue must be realistic
   * the dialogue must have a beginning, middle, and end
   * the dialogue must be set up in a play or dialogue format
   * add extra space between each character's lines to allow for easier script reading

4. Once the pairs have completed their duologs, have each pair ask another pair to read their duolog out loud to them. Tell the writers to evaluate their duolog based on the following criteria and then revise it:
   * Does it make sense?
   * Does it sound natural and realistic?
   * Are there lines or words that need changing?
   * What needs to be added or deleted?

5. Have each pair make three copies of their duolog and give one to you for evaluation.

6. Assign oral presentations. The pair who wrote the duolog is also presenting it. Remind the groups that you will evaluate them on: eye contact, smoothness of delivery, rate, expression, and volume.

7. You may want to use the Warm-Up Exercises in Appendix 7 before groups make their presentations.

Teacher Tips

1. You may let the students choose their subjects, but make sure that the duologs do not contain offensive material before they are performed.

2. You could assign each student a particular character from a literary work. For example, they could craft a dialogue between the two fathers in *Romeo and Juliet*.

3. You could assign each student a historical character to depict in the dialogue, e.g., Lincoln chats with Washington about slavery.

Evaluation

You can assign grades based on the written work and the performance, using the Duolog Evaluation Form.

Your Basic Quaddie

A Sample Duolog

"Could you believe what Stacey was wearing today?"

"Oh gawd! I know! She looked like such a sleaze!"

"Well, that's 'cause she is! Didn't you hear about her and that guy in Biology?"

"Which guy?"

"That totally cute one that sits in back."

"Oh, him! He's soo rad!"

"Yeah, well, they did IT!"

"Reeally?"

"Yea, she's a total wench!"

"Gee, I guess so!"

"Well, I don't wanna talk about that sleaze anymore. Don't you think John is sooo cute!"

"Hey, yes! And he has, like, this totally awesome body!"

"What happened to David?"

"Oh, him. He doesn't even have a car. We had to ride in his mom's station wagon everywhere. It was, like, soo embarrassing!"

"What kinda car does John have?"

"A BMW! It's soo hot! I'm soo glad I broke up with David yesterday!"

"Oh, gawd! Here comes that slimebag Stacy!"

"Oh, I know. Look at the way she walks!"

"Ooh, hii, Stacey! How are you? I loove your dress! It, like, totally fits your personality!"

Duolog Evaluation Form

Manuscript Evaluation

Names _____ _____

	Publish It!	Minor Revisions	Acceptable	Needs Work	Try Again	Comments
Information about names, setting, and action come from the dialogue.	5	4	3	2	I	
Realistic dialogue	5	4	3	2	I	
Story has clear beginning, middle, and end.	5	4	3	2	I	
Manuscript is in clear form and three copies have been made.	5	4	3	2	I	

Oral Evaluation

Names _____ _____

Eye contact w/ partner	5	4	3	2	I
Well-rehearsed	5	4	3	2	I
Volume/projection	5	4	3	2	I
Vocal variety	5	4	3	2	I
Rate	5	4	3	2	I
Emotional content	5	4	3	2	I
Obvious teamwork	5	4	3	2	I

Oral Interpretation of a Biography/Autobiography

An activity designed to present biographical information with students speaking in character.

Materials

biography or autobiography
Biography/Autobiography Assignment Sheet
Biography/ Autobiography Written Report
Sample Outline for an Informative Speech (page 66)
Oral Interpretation of Biography/Autobiography Evaluation Form
Self-Evaluation of Oral Biography/Autobiography
Appendix 7: Warm Up Exercises (optional)

Procedure

1. Tell the students that they will be presenting speeches in character based on a biography or an autobiography. You may assign specific books or allow the students to choose them from a suggested list.
2. Distribute the Biography/Autobiography Assignment and Written Report sheets and review them with the class.
3. Ask the students to read the book and write a report covering the points outlined in the Biography/Autobiography Written Report.
4. Have the students write outlines for their presentations. The Sample Outline for an Informative Speech is a useful example.
5. Schedule student presentations.
6. If the speakers need invigorating, employ the Warm Up Exercises from Appendix 7.
7. Distribute the Oral Interpretation of Biography/Autobiography Evaluation Form and explain the criteria for evaluation.
8. Once the students have finished their presentations, ask them to complete the Self-Evaluation of Oral Biography/Autobiography.

Teacher Tips

You may want to have the students develop a visual image of their character, giving their presentation in suitable costume with appropriate props.

Evaluation

You can grade the written report, outline, and oral presentation using the Oral Interpretation of Biography/ Autobiography Evaluation Form.

Biography/Autobiography Assignment Sheet

1. Select a biography/autobiography.

2. Read the book!

3. Compose a written report (see Biography/Autobiography Written Report).

4. Prepare an outline that will help you present this person to the class. The divisions in the body of the outline are up to you, but consider chronological order and/or family background, formal/informal education, contribution to mankind, impact on society, etc.

5. Present the report to the class by becoming the character you have studied. Use the information developed on the outline. If appropriate, wear your costume and use your props so that the audience really gets the feel of the character. The report should be between 4–6 minutes.

6. Remember you are the star!

Paper Due _____

Outline Due_____

Speeches Begin _____

Biography/Autobiography Written Report

I. **Publication Information** (you may just list)
- title
- author
- date of publication
- number of pages
- name of person being studied

II. **About the Book** (please respond in complete sentences and paragraphs for the rest of the paper)
- summary (Don't try to tell us everything—keep it brief.)
- conflicts (Include page #'s with quotes to support who/what/why.)
- solutions (What solutions come up or fail to surface?)
- time (When in history did/does the person live?)
- place (Where does the person live?)
- significance of time/place (What events in the person's life were shaped by the time and place in which they happened?)

III. **Theme of a Person's Life**
- cause of prominence (What led to this person's fame?)
- turning points (What experiences, ideas, or self-realizations caused this person to change?)
- theme of person's life (How would you sum up the controlling idea of the person's life?
- what you learned (What did you learn about life by reading about this person?)

IV. **Point of View**
- Is the narrator's point of view first person ("I") or third person ("she/he")?
- Is this a primary or secondary source?
- Does it have a subjective or objective viewpoint?
- What difference does point of view make to the story?

V. **Evaluation**
- Write one well-developed paragraph expressing your personal evaluation of the book.
- What did you learn from it?
- Was it worthwhile?
- Support your point of view with examples.

Oral Interpretation of Biography/Autobiography Evaluation Form

Name_____ Person_____

	Fantastic!	Above Average	Good	Needs Revision	Try Again!	Comments
Voice and body language	5	4	3	2	1	
Eye contact with audience	5	4	3	2	1	
Vocal projection	5	4	3	2	1	
Character fully developed	5	4	3	2	1	
Use of props and/or costumes	5	4	3	2	1	

Self-Evaluation of Oral Biography/Autobiography

Name_____ Period _____

1. Name your book and its author.

2. How well do you think you portrayed your character?

3. How much did you practice? Would more have helped?

4. Give a justification for what grade you think you deserve.

Persuasion Without Rhetoric

An exercise in persuasion that takes a text void of rhetoric and
adds body movement and voice to make it look and sound persuasive.

Materials

math or science text book
Tips for Performers
Persuasion Without Rhetoric Scoring Guide

Procedure

1. Ask the students to copy two sentences from a math or science textbook. Stress that the sentences must be void of rhetoric.
2. Tell them that they will be delivering their sentences to the class from memory, but first they can practice in groups.
3. Divide the class into coaching groups to practice their material. Encourage the groups to coach and give feedback to each member.
4. Distribute and review Tips for Performers.
5. Hand out and review the criteria of assessment in the Persuasion Without Rhetoric Scoring Guide.
6. Schedule the presentations. Each individual in each coaching group performs in front of the class for a grade. (Everyone's allowed one "choke" for only a 2-point penalty.)

Evaluation

Complete the Persuasion Without Rhetoric Scoring Guide for each student.
Optional: The coaching group with the highest cumulative score earns ten bonus points.

Tips for Performers

Do	Don't
stand and move with poise	step backwards/shift weight
have eye-contact with audience	look at the ceiling, floor, wall
use effective hand gestures	smirk
use appropriate facial expressions	have hand contact with your body (e.g., don't play with your hair)

Persuasion Without Rhetoric Scoring Guide

Name_____ Period _____

	Got It!	Almost	What?
Pronunciation (Saying the words correctly)	3	2	1
Enunciation (Saying the words clearly)	3	2	1
Inflection (Emphasizing the right words)	3	2	1
Rate (Pausing in the right places)	3	2	1
Body language (Proper movement, eye contact, gestures)	3	2	1

Comments on overall persuasive impact:

Storytelling

An experience that develops speaking and listening skills
while encouraging the exchange of cultural/ethnic heritages.

Materials

Storytelling Group Student Practice and Procedure
Storytelling Scoring Guide

Procedure

1. Give some background on storytelling and/or tell a story to the class.
2. Give the students guidelines in storytelling including:
   a. Character dialogue should never be summarized. It need not be memorized word-for-word, but the characters should speak (i.e., The hen said, "Get out of here!" *not* "The hen told the fox to leave.").
   b. The moral at the end of a fable must be memorized accurately.
3. Secure several copies of various fables.
4. Divide the class into equal groups. Distribute a different fable to each group.
5. Introduce Storytelling Group Student Practice and Procedure.
6. Move among the groups as they work.
7. To avoid over-memorization, do not allow the students to take the copies home.
8. Hear group presentations.
9. Schedule individual presentations and tell the students to follow the steps for individual student practice for homework.

Evaluation

Use the Storytelling Scoring Guide to evaluate the students.

Storytelling Group Student Practice and Procedure

1. **Read the Fable Silentlly:** Each member of the group reads the fable silently.

2. **Read the Fable Aloud:** One group member at a time may read a section; one can read the narration and others can read characters. ALL must be involved in the reading. Read the fable a minimum of two times.

3. **Discuss:** Discuss the fable with major emphasis on the sequence of events and the meaning of the fable.

4. **Read Aloud Again:** Share the reading again, allowing time for at least two read-throughs. Remember that stories are easier to understand when we hear them several times!

5. **Flesh Out:** Talk about the characters' attitudes, their dialogue, the appropriate voice for each character, images in the fable, and the setting of the fable.

6. **Group Tell:** Place the fable face down on your desk. One group member should start the fable, using dialogue where appropriate. Stop. Let the next person pick up where you left off and continue in this way until the fable is finished. All members repeat the moral.

7. **Individual "Tell the Wall":** Stand and face a wall with at least an arm's length between you and the person next to you. (All members of your group should be at the same wall; do not mix groups.) DO NOT take a copy of the fable with you. Practice telling the entire fable to the wall.

8. **Sharing the Fable:** Now, change groups so that each group has an A, B, C, and D member. Tell your fable to the other members of the new group. DO NOT use your script.

9. **Presentation:** Reunite with your original group. Your teacher will ask you to step outside and come into the room, one at a time, to present your fable. The listeners will critique each person.

Individual Student Practice and Procedure:

1. Locate a story, fable, tale, myth, or legend to present on your own.

2. Using the process for preparing to tell a story and what you learned in the group practice, prepare to present the story to the class.

3. Present your tale to the class, with a short introduction that includes the title, author, and source of your tale. You may wish to include the background of the story or the reason for choosing it.

4. Provide a copy for the teacher.

Storytelling Scoring Guide

Name_____ Period_____ Date_____

Story/Fable/Tale/Myth/Legend_____

	Exceptional Achievement	Adequate Achievement	Some Evidence of Achievement	Limited Evidence of Achievement	Comments
Use of Characters (Use of specific dialogue)	5	4	3	2 / 1	
Physical Involvement (Gestures, movement, facial expression, eye contact)	5	4	3	2 / 1	
Vocal Involvement (Volume, rate, diction, feeling, emphasis)	5	4	3	2 / 1	
Narration (Story easy to follow, exciting)	5	4	3	2 / 1	
Overall Effect (Does the total performance make the story exciting/funny/dramatic/ come alive, etc.?)	5	4	3	2 / 1	

Comments:

Did You Say That?

A speaking activity emphasizing inflection

Materials
Did You Say That? Sample Exercises

Procedure
You can assign this either as an individual or group activity.

Individual Activity
1. Read the sentence "I didn't tell John you were stupid" aloud several times, each time emphasizing a different word in the sentence.
2. Ask the students for the meaning of each sentence as you change emphasis.
3. Assign each student a sentence and a desired meaning, and ask the student to read the sentence with the emphasis on the correct word to bring out the meaning assigned.

Group Activity
1. Read the sentence "I didn't tell John you were stupid" aloud several times, each time emphasizing a different word in the sentence.
2. Discuss the meaning of each sentence as you change emphasis.
3. Assign each group a sentence and several meanings.
4. Tell the students to work together to determine the emphasis that provides the correct meaning. (Allow a fixed amount of time, say 10–15 minutes, for this.)
5. Ask each student in a group to read the sentence using emphasis to obtain one of the assigned meanings.
6. Ask the other groups for the meaning of each sentence as the student reads it.

Teacher Tips
1. Consider warming up the students with Did You Say That? Sample Exercises.
2. Suggested meanings for "I didn't tell John you were stupid."

<u>I</u> didn't tell John you were stupid.	*(Someone else told him.)*
I <u>didn't</u> tell John you were stupid.	*(I'm keeping the fact a secret.)*
I didn't <u>tell</u> John you were stupid.	*(I only hinted at it.)*
I didn't tell <u>John</u> you were stupid.	*(I told everyone but John.)*
I didn't tell John <u>you</u> were stupid.	*(I said someone around here was stupid. John figured it out by himself.)*
I didn't tell John you <u>were</u> stupid.	*(I told him you still are stupid.)*
I didn't tell John you were <u>stupid</u>.	*(I merely voiced my conviction that you weren't very bright.)*

Evaluation
1. Give students points for using the proper emphasis on the first try; fewer points for a second try.
2. In the group activity, you may grade students individually.

Did You Say That? Sample Exercises

You could use the following examples to obtain the indicated meaning by a change in inflection.

Yes, I like her.

She is probably all right, but I am not eager for her friendship

I'd better say I like her, but I don't believe it.

I'm sure of it.

Whatever others think, she suits me.

I like her, though my friend does not.

I like her, but no more than that.

I like her, but not the other girl

Who said I did not?

I think she is a fine girl.

She's wonderful.

I thought he would fail.

And he has.

Just what I expected all along.

What a mistake I made.

I cannot understand why he hasn't.

How absurd.

Ironically. When obviously he hasn't.

But I don't think it would matter.

But I wasn't prepared for such a complete failure.

But others didn't.

But I wasn't sure.

But not the others.

She saw me.

Asking a question.

Pleased surprise.

Horrified surprise.

Stout affirmation.

Sarcasm.

Oh, he did?

Surprise.

Threat. You'll see about it.

Fear.

Jeering.

You were wonderful.

Warmly.

He was good; the others were bad.

He used to be good but isn't anymore.

Surprised he wasn't pretty bad.

Pleased to learn that he was a success.

He really was pretty bad.

SECTION VIII
Spontaneous Speaking

Spontaneous speaking activities allow students to ease into the demands of making an oral presentation while giving them the real-life experience of thinking and speaking on their feet. Spontaneous speaking can serve as warm-up exercises, can help with the understanding of literature across the curriculum, and can prepare students to make oral presentations.

Impromptu Speaking

An exercise teaching students how to construct, deliver, and
evaluate short impromptu speeches on a variety of topics.

Materials

Impromptu Speech Reference Sheet
Impromptu Speech Scoring Guide
Impromptu Sample Topics (optional)
Appendix 7: Warm Up Exercises (optional)

Procedure

1. Distribute the Impromptu Speech Reference Sheet and discuss the elements of impromptu speaking.
2. Hand out the Impromptu Speech Scoring Guide and review.
3. Tell the students that they will have a given amount of time (perhaps 2–5 minutes) to prepare and a given amount of time to speak (2–5 minutes works best).
4. To alleviate anxiety, employ the warm up exercises from Appendix 7 before the first speaker draws a topic.
5. Give each speaker a topic slip containing one of the following: three words, three quotations, or three topics of current interest. For example:

   Abstract Words
   - Hate
   - Anger
   - Fear

   Quotations
   - "That's one small step for (a) man, one giant leap for mankind." (Neil Armstrong)
   - "Never look back—something might be gaining on you." (Satchel Paige)
   - "Ask not what your country can do for you, ask what you can do for your country." (John F. Kennedy)

   Topics of Current Interest
   - Should the federal government give financial aide to victims of natural disasters?
   - Should Supreme Court justices be elected?
   - Have high school proms become too extravagant?
6. Ask each student to speak on *one* of the topics on their topic slip.

Teacher Tips

Here are two alternate methods of generating the topics:

1. Have the students write five topics related to the upcoming exam and submit them to you for approval. Write the topics on separate strips of paper. On presentation day, have each student draw one of his/her five topics to speak on. Alternatively, all of the approved topics could be placed in a large hat or box and each student draw from the collective pool of topics.
2. You choose the topics. Write three to six topics on the board. Give each student a chance to write a short speech on one of the topics. Have the students present their speeches. They may use their script if desired.

Evaluation

Use the Impromptu Scoring Guide to evaluate the speeches.

Impromptu Speech Reference Sheet

Definition of Impromptu
An impromptu speech is a short speech, varying in length, with little or no specific preparation. The speaker may or may not be an expert on the topic. The speech includes an attention getter, thesis, main points and conclusion.

Speech Format
An impromptu speech follows the same format as other speeches:

1. **Introduction:** Include attention getting device and thesis. You may want to give a sign-posting sentence. For example, "We are going to look at this topic in the following three ways: yaba, dabba, and doo." Attention getter:
   - a brief story/anecdote
   - a relevant joke or humorous story
   - a startling fact or quotation
   - a personal experience
2. **Body:** Discuss main points. Main points should cover two to four main ideas leading to the conclusion. Give examples, facts, stories, whatever you can. Always expand and prove your ideas, but don't wander. Personal stories are always good if credible and relevant.
3. **Conclusion:** Reference the attention getter, perhaps resolving it, summarize the main points or call for action. Your speech has taken us on a journey. Restate the introduction, but take into account what we've learned along the way.
4. **End:** Say what you planned to say and sit down, even if your speech is too short. You don't need to get repetitious. It's quality, not quantity.

Preparation tips
1. Choose your topic quickly. Once you decide, don't change.
2. Develop a general thesis statement. Decide what main idea you want to convey to your audience.
3. Pick out two to four points to develop your thesis. This is where you determine your organization. You may want to use one of the following types of organization:
   - **Problem-Solution:** discuss a problem, then show the possible solutions.
   - **Effect-Causes:** discuss the situation, then tell what caused it.
   - **Past-Present-Future:** discuss past highlights, the present situation, and possible future developments.
   - **Chronological:** discuss your subject as it happened through history or through time.

- **Myself-My Neighbors/Friends-Mankind:** progress from specific to general.
- **City-State-National-International:** progress from specific to general.
- **Pendulum Swing:** show one extreme and then show how we have swung to the other extreme.
- **Journalistic:** Answer the who, what, where, when, how, and why questions.
- **Situation:** Define the situation and explain its pros and cons.
- **Impact:** Discuss political, social, economic implications.
- **Need-Plan-Advantages:** Identify the need, outline a plan, present advantages of implementation.

4. Decide on an attention-getting device for your introduction. Stories, illustrations, quotations and personal experiences are always good.

5. Select concrete examples to demonstrate each of your main points.

Impromptu Speech Scoring Guide

Name_____ Period_____ Date_____

Topic _____

	Got it!	Almost	What?	Comments
Introduction (attention getter/thesis statement)	3	2	I	
Main Points (2–4 points with support)	3	2	I	
Conclusion (summary, restatement, etc.)	3	2	I	
Physical Delivery (eye contact, gestures, posture)	3	2	I	
Vocal Delivery (volume, diction, rate)	3	2	I	

Comments:

Impromptu Sample Topics

Abstract Words Topic Sheet

✂--

character
approval
tardiness

✂--

fate
punishment
symbolism

✂--

blame
kindness
opinion

✂--

malice
consensus
persuasion

✂--

responsibility
future
success

✂--

corruption
initiative
legacy

✂--

champion
sarcasm
guarantee

✂--

criticism
generosity
fun

✂--

jealousy
intent
warmth

✂--

hope
risk
ethics

✂--

empathy
boredom
surprise

✂--

Obscure Words Topic Sheet

✂- -

adactylous
busk
carious

✂- -

defalcate
elusion
flocculent

✂- -

goffer
hanse
isocracy

✂- -

jo
knacker
lictor

✂- -

maieutic
naumachia
oodles

✂- -

porism
quatorze
relume

✂- -

sere
testudo
urtication

✂- -

vaticinal
winze
xiphoid

✂- -

yogh
zymotic
mazzard

✂- -

Quotations Topic Sheet

✂--

"I think I can. I think I can. I think I can." (*Little Engine That Could*, Watty Piper)

"Dear me! What a troublesome business a family is!" (*Water-Babies*, Charles Kingsley)

"You have brains in your head. You have feet in your shoes. You can steer yourself any direction you choose." (*Oh, the Places You'll Go!*, Dr. Seuss)

✂--

"You must not hop on Pop." (*Hop on Pop*, Dr. Seuss)

"A good detective is always in demand." (*Nancy Drew Mystery Series: The Hidden Staircase*, Carolyn Keene)

"To die will be an awfully big adventure." (*Peter Pan*, J.M.Barrie)

✂--

"Safety is well and good: I prefer freedom." (*Trumpet of the Swan*, E.B. White)

"Everything's got a moral, if only you can find it" (*Alice in Wonderland*, Lewis Carroll)

"True friends never owe each other anything." (*Bear Circus*, William Pene Du Bois)

✂--

"Nothing ever seems interesting when it belongs to you—only when it doesn't" (*Tuck Everlasting*, Natalie Babbit)

"Every night the river sings a new song." (*Land of Right Up and Down*, Eva-Lis Wuorio)

"Grownups sure do a lot of pretending and call it politeness." (*Miss Charity Comes to Stay*, Albert Wilson Constant)

✂--

"Dark ain't so bad if you know what's in it" (*Whipping Boy*, Sid Fleischman)

"To fear is one thing. To let fear grab you by the tail and swing you around is another." (*Jacob Have I Loved*, Katherine Paterson)

"I wish we had tails to wag,' said Mr. Dearly." (*101 Dalmations*, Dodie Smith)

✂--

"What fantastic creatures boys are." (*Charlotte's Web*, E.B. White)

"If some things were different, other things would be otherwise." (*Griffin and the Minor Canon*, Frank Stockton)

"It is ever so much easier to be good if your clothes are fashionable" (*Anne of Green Gables*, L.M. Montgomery)

✂--

"Pride comes before the fall." (*Æsop's Fables*)

"Things are not untrue just because they never happened." (*Hare's Choices*, Dannis Hamley)

"So many, many things are Mystery." (*Emily*, Michael Bedard)

✂--

Current Interest Topic Sheet

✂- -

Should capital punishment be abolished?

Should the president of the United States be elected by a direct vote of the people?

Should the federal government provide national healthcare?

✂- -

Should college athletes be paid?

Do beauty pageants do more harm than good?

Is television a bad influence?

✂- -

Should schools require uniforms?

Should the voting age be lowered to sixteen?

Should cell phones with cameras be banned from schools?

✂- -

Should all 18 year old US citizens be required to perform 2 years of national service?

Are genetically modified foods a health threat?

Should all children be immunized?

✂- -

Do school lunch programs meet children's nutritional needs?

Should professional athletes be randomly drug tested?

Should the legal driving age be raised to 18 years?

✂- -

Are the advantages of "wired" hospitals worth the costs and the risks?

Should drivers over the age of 65 be more rigorously tested for competence?

Should SUVs be taxed as a luxury item?

Off the Top of Your Head

An exercise to help students organize and outline personal examples around
a central idea before giving an impromptu speech or writing an essay.

Materials

Off the Top of Your Head Sample Exercise
Off the Top of Your Head Sample Outline
Off the Top of Your Head Assignment Sheet
Impromptu Speech Scoring Guide (page 220)

Procedure

1. Give the students 10 minutes to list "what's on the top of your head." Have them consider current events, recent films, books studied in class, personal experiences, and decisions. They may list as many items as they want; the only limiting factor is the time. Distribute Off the Top of Your Head Sample Exercise to help illustrate the activity. Give each student a copy of the Off the Top of Your Head Assignment Sheet.

2. When the list is complete, give students an abstract word. Their essay or oral presentation will be organized around this abstract word and their list.

3. Give the students 5 minutes to comb their list for connections to the abstract word.

4. After the students have made connections between their list and their abstract word, ask them to formulate a controlling idea.

5. Give the students 10 minutes to outline their potential essay or presentation. Review the criteria for assessment in the Impromptu Speech Scoring Guide.

Teacher Tips

1. You may want to help students generate their list by prompting them with questions (e.g., What was the last movie you saw? Which book are you reading in English class?).

2. You may want to give more than one abstract word and allow the students to choose one.

3. Students may present their completed outlines as impromptu speeches or utilize the outlines for essays.

4. If the assignment is repeated, you may want to challenge the students with less prep time for the outline.

Evaluation

See the Impromptu Speech Scoring Guide for evaluating oral presentations.

Off the Top of Your Head Sample Exercise

Step One:

Off the top of your head, list what's on your mind (consider current events, recent films, books being studied in class, personal experiences and decisions).

lack of sleep

Gladiator

To Kill a Mockingbird

the prom

car payment/insurance

lunch

Presidential scandal

Interview With a Vampire

school violence

Austin Powers

tanning

unfair curfew

the Vietnam War

entropy

N'Sync

grades

baseball playoffs

mom's birthday

The Simpsons

Step Two:

Abstract word (given by the teacher when the list is complete): justice

Step Three:

Comb your list for connections to the abstract word.

Gladiator

To Kill a Mockingbird

car payment/insurance

school violence

unfair curfew

grades

Step Four:

Formulate a controlling idea or thesis.

Teenagers are denied justice on issues ranging from grades to violence.

Step Five:

Outline your potential essay or presentation.

Off the Top of Your Head Sample Outline

Introduction
Personal example describing an argument with parents about Saturday's curfew

Controlling Idea or Thesis
Teenagers are denied justice on issues ranging from grades to violence.

Main Points

    I. High schoolers have no recourse when faced with an unjust grade.
        A. Grades in many subjects, such as English and art, are subjective.
        B. Teachers' grading policies are often unclear and inconsistent.

    II. In *To Kill a Mockingbird*, Mayella has no recourse against her father's abuse.
        A. She was too young to be taken seriously.
        B. She was too poor to garner respect.

    III. Many acts of school violence go unpunished.
        A. Hazing and harassment often go unreported.
        B. Punishment for reported incidents is often inconsistent.

Conclusion
Teenagers have no recourse when faced with unfair situations.

Off the Top of Your Head Assignment Sheet

Step One: Off the top of your head, list what's on your mind (consider current events, recent films, books being studied in class, personal experiences and decisions).

Step Two: Abstract word (given by the teacher when the list is complete).

Step Three: Comb your list for connections to the abstract word.

Step Four: Formulate a controlling idea or thesis.

Step Five: Outline your potential essay or presentation.

Introduction

Controlling Idea or Thesis

Main Points

    I.

        A.

        B.

    II.

        A.

        B.

    III.

        A.

        B.

Conclusion

Sixty Seconds: An Impromptu Game

An exercise to help students work on the articulation and delivery of impromptu speeches.

Materials
Impromptu Speech Reference Sheet (page 218)

Procedure
1. Follow basic procedure for Impromptu Speaking found on page 217.
2. Decide which particular skill you want practiced and review it with the students.
3. Explain to the students that they will be giving impromptu speeches on teacher-selected topics to practice this skill.
4. Distribute and discuss Impromptu Speech Reference Sheet.
5. Outline the rules for the speeches. For example, students will be marked down for:
   - Hesitation, including non-fluencies (such as "uh" or lapses of three seconds)
   - Deviation from the rules of grammar or standard English
   - Unnecessary words (such as "like" or "y'know")
   - Error in factual accuracy or the use of subject matter knowledge
   - Violation of these rules becomes grounds for a challenge during the activity.
6. Divide the students into groups of four (or whatever may be convenient). Designate one member in each group Speaker One. The first speaker from Group A speaks on the subject for as long as he/she can, up to 60 seconds, without violating any of the rules you have outlined.
7. Any other Speaker One who detects a violation may "tag" the violator by issuing a challenge, which temporarily stops the clock. If you decide the challenge is valid, the challenger takes over and speaks in the remaining time (subject to further challenges).
8. Once the first 60-second period is completed, Speaker One from Group B begins to speak. Once all the first speakers have had their turn, the second speakers from all groups get their turn. Only Speaker Ones can challenge other Speaker Ones, and so forth. Speakers may speak by successfully challenging another speaker, but they must still speak when it is their turn to give their 60-second presentation.

Teacher Tips
Unusual topics may be effective in some classrooms. Use obscure words whose definition no one could possibly know, and then challenge the students to invent plausible definitions. Nonsense quotations are a good means of challenging students to be creative. Throw students a "curve" by asking questions that have no connection to real life, e.g., "Are feather dusters or nail polish more essential to life on Mars?"

Evaluation
1. You may want to use the following scoring system:
   - The speaker who is speaking at the conclusion of 60 seconds receives one point.
   - A speaker who is incorrectly challenged receives an additional point.
   - A speaker who speaks for the full 60 seconds without being challenged successfully receives an additional two points.
2. You may award points for accurate or extensive use of subject matter studied.

Generic Job Interview

An exercise to help students respond spontaneously to job interview questions with articulate, thorough answers.

Materials

Generic Job History
Generic Job Interview Questions
Generic Job Interview Scoring Guide

Procedure

1. Assign an individual or a panel of students to interview a series of students for a generic job.
2. Ask the interviewees to prepare the Generic Job History. And give both the interviewers and the interviewees copies of Generic Job Interview Questions to prepare them for their interviews.
3. Schedule the interviews. Each interview should last 5–10 minutes.

Teacher Tips

1. Student or teacher may choose a particular job for which the interviewee is applying.
2. You can tailor questions to fit a particular area of expertise—such as computer programming, business management, etc.
3. You can ask applicants to bring a portfolio of their work to the interview.
4. You can ask applicants to develop their real resume for the interview.
5. Remind students to consider babysitting, being captain of a team, and being a teacher's assistant as past job experience on the Generic Job History.
6. You may want to instruct the students on proper etiquette for a job interview, including appropriate dress and manners (e.g., how to shake hands, sit in the chair, etc.).

Evaluation

Have the interviewers complete the Generic Job Interview Scoring Guide for the interviewee.

Generic Job History

Name_____Grade_____

Current job experience:

Past job experience (in reverse chronological order):

Duties performed on previous jobs:

Personal strengths and weaknesses:

Long-range career goals:

Hobbies and other interests:

Generic Job Interview Questions

1. Why do you want a full/part-time job?

2. What are your strengths?

3. What are your weaknesses?

4. What hours can you work?

5. Please describe your job experiences?

6. What do you like most about this time in your life?

7. What do you like least about this time in your life?

8. What do you consider your greatest educational achievement?

9. What do you consider your greatest accomplishment?

10. Do you work hard for grades, or do grades come naturally without a lot of effort?

11. Which courses interest you the most and the least? Why?

12. What are your future educational goals?

13. Please tell us about the kinds of people you most enjoy working with.

14. Please describe the responsibilities of your present or last job.

15. How would you describe your ideal job?

16. What is the biggest source of job satisfaction for you?

17. How busy do you like to be in your job?

18. How do you respond when circumstances require that you change your work plans or schedule? Can you give me an example?

19. What attributes do you possess that will make you successful?

20. Please tell me about a time at work or school when you felt motivated.

21. Describe a situation that demonstrates your level of motivation. How do you maintain this level?

22. Describe an occasion at work or school that you found discouraging.

23. Please describe an occasion when a major obstacle was in the way of your accomplishing a major goal. How did you handle the situation?

24. Sometimes it is difficult to know when to quit. Describe an experience when you were too persistent or not persistent enough.

25. Please describe a significant effort on which you worked as part of a team to accomplish a mutual goal. Was it successful?

Generic Job Interview Scoring Guide

Name (interviewee) _____

	Hired!	Call Back	Wait List	Don't Call Us, We'll Call You
Quality of Responses				
Thoroughness	5	4	3	2 / 1
Organization	5	4	3	2 / 1
Sincerity	5	4	3	2 / 1
Quality of Expression				
Enthusiasm/ energy	5	4	3	2 / 1
Clear articulation	5	4	3	2 / 1
Eye contact	5	4	3	2 / 1
Appearance	5	4	3	2 / 1

Spontaneous Fishbowl Debate

An experience that develops speaking and listening skills while encouraging the exchange of ideas through arguments.

Materials

Fishbowl Participants Scoring Guide
Appendix 1: How to Select a Topic and Present It in a Resolution Format

Procedure

1. Generate a list of debatable topics based on a piece of literature or subject matter assigned. (See Appendix 1: How to Select a Topic and Present It in a Resolution Format.)
2. Place the students' desks in a large circle around the classroom.
3. Place two to six empty desks in the middle of the circle (within the "fishbowl"), half of the desks facing the other half. The Pros will sit on one side, while the Cons sit on the other.
4. Assign students to the Pro and Con views and discuss the criteria for evaluation in the Fishbowl Participants Scoring Guide. You may give the students a few minutes to prepare.
5. Give each individual a set time, such as two minutes, for opening statements and responses. Debate alternates between opposing sides.
6. The rest of the class listens carefully to the debate and takes notes to offer constructive evaluations of the debaters at the completion of the activity.
7. When a debater in the fishbowl runs out of things to say, he/she gets up from the center desk, moves to a desk in the outside circle, and any student from the outside circle takes his/her place and continues the debate.
8. When a student in the outside circle is anxious to take the place of one of the debaters he/she stands next to the individual he/she wishes to replace.

Teacher Tips

1. To extend participation, students on the outside of the fishbowl can:
   • ask questions of debaters to receive points.
   • take notes on the discussion and receive points for the accuracy of their notes.

Evaluation

Use Fishbowl Participants Scoring Guide to assess the students.

Fishbowl Participants Scoring Guide

	Exceptional	Proficient	Basic
Delivery (Communicative and persuasive in manner)	3	2	I
Original Arguments (New or innovative views on the issue)	3	2	I
Clash (Directly responds to the issues presented)	3	2	I
Analysis (Logical examination of the issues)	3	2	I

Tableau

An experience that develops analysis of character, plot, and theme through speaking and listening skills.

Materials

Tableau Scoring Guide
Appendix 7: Warm Up Exercises (optional)

Procedure

1. Divide the class into groups of four to six.
2. Assign a scene from a piece of literature or historical event to each group. Students may select a significant scene on their own.

   Sample Scenes

   Art: when studying periods or movements in art
   Example: the commissioning of Michelangelo to paint the Sistine Chapel

   English: when using any piece of literature
   Example: Brave New World: scene with Lenina and Bernard on the reservation

   Modern Language: when using literature in the language being studied or when studying different historical or present-day events
   Example: the storming of the Bastille

   Music: when studying periods or styles in music
   Example: Francis Scott Key writing the Star Spangled Banner

   Science/Math: when studying concepts
   Example: Einstein developing the theory of relativity

   Social Studies: when studying historical or current events
   Example: the signing of the Declaration of Independence

3. Ask the students in each group to discuss the possible actions and motivations of each character or figure for the assigned moment and determine who will enact each role.
4. Ask the groups to determine the pose (tableau) that they wish to be in when their scene opens.
5. Review the criteria for assessment in Tableau Scoring Guide.
6. If the speakers need invigorating, employ the warm up exercises from Appendix 7.
7. Have the groups take turns performing for the entire class using the following guidelines:
   - The performance begins with each actor frozen, holding a pose and unable to speak.
   - The teacher signals students when they are to speak by tapping them, once to start and twice to stop. Students may speak and move only when tapped and must continue speaking until tapped again.
   - Each student speaks the thoughts of the character he/she is enacting. The conversation resembles "stream of consciousness" thinking. Students improvise based on their understanding of the characters.
   - Multiple characters may be unfrozen at one time but do not have dialogue with each other.

Teacher Tips

1. If using a literary work, students may choose to do a scene not in the work but implied by the content, or they may choose to do a scene they wish the author had included.

2. As a variation, you can unfreeze multiple characters at the same time so that the students will have a dialogue with each other.

Evaluation

Use the Tableau Scoring Guide to assess the presentations.

Tableau Scoring Guide

	Academy Award	Nominated for Award	Expect Call Back	Nice Try	Don't Call Us; We'll Call You!	Comments
Eye Contact	5	4	3	2	1	
Stays in Character	5	4	3	2	1	
Volume/ Projection	5	4	3	2	1	
Vocal Variety	5	4	3	2	1	
Rate (speed of delivery)	5	4	3	2	1	
Content (consistent with literary work or historical perspective)	5	4	3	2	1	

Appendixes

Appendix 1: How to Select a Topic and Present It in a Resolution Format

Topics should be controversial, balanced, and made in positive form (avoiding "not"). The wording should be kept simple and clear.

Make sure your topic is . . .

Controversial—that there are reasonable arguments on both sides of the issue.
- good controversial topic: *Resolved that uniforms should be required in public high schools*
- poor controversial topic: *Resolved that we should have less crime in the United States.*

Balanced—that there is equal ground for each side to debate.
- well-balanced topic: *Resolved that the death penalty should be abolished in the United States.*
- poorly-balanced (one-sided) topic: *Resolved that sports should be abolished in high school.*

Make sure your resolution is . . .

Worded as a value or policy *not* **a fact** (fact topics can lead to dead-end debates if one side lacks evidence).

There are three types of resolutions:
- Value: *Resolved that individuals have the right to smoke.*
  A value-based resolution uses a qualifying word and places one value over another.
- Policy: *Resolved that cigarette smoking should be abolished in all public facilities in the United States.*
  A policy-based resolution advocates a change in current policy.
- Fact: *Resolved that cigarette smoking is hazardous to human health.*
  A fact-based resolution can be proven true or false based on evidence.

Value and Policy topics work best in the classroom in a positive form (avoiding "not," which lends itself to confusion since debaters in favor of an issue will have to go against its resolution.)
- Positive Form: *Resolved that academics are more important than extra-curricular activities.*
- Negative Form: *Resolved that all students should not be required to participate in extra-curricular activities.*

Appendix 2: How to Ask and Answer Questions in a Debate

Some debate formats incorporate time for question and answer periods. These can be the best part of a debate, as question time is interactive and can be very entertaining and informative. You will not automatically sparkle in question and answer time. You must learn and practice the skills for asking and answering questions, just like any other skill.

Strive to Ask Questions That Require . . .

Clarification

"What do you mean by the term 'racial bias'?"

Interpretation

"What's in the evidence to show that capital punishment had anything to do with the murder rate in California?"

Speculation

"If capital punishment were replaced with life sentences, how would the criminal justice system be affected?"

Application

"How would you feel if one of your family members were murdered?"

Analysis

"How do you explain the fact that the murder rate drops following an execution?"

Avoid . . .

Questions that can be answered yes/no

"Does California currently have a death penalty?"

Friendly questions

"Do you agree that the death penalty is wrong?"

Tips on Cross-Examination

- Limit the number of arguments you ask your opponent to restate.
- Do not back down too soon.
- Keep the exchange even. Don't permit the respondent to talk the time away. If you must interrupt, do so gracefully, e.g., "Thanks, I understand."
- Tell the truth when you know it. Never deny the obvious or lie.
- Stay calm. Stay in control of your emotions and you will appear confident.

Appendix 3: Constructing a Speech for a Debate

In a debate, a speaker presents arguments and supporting evidence for or against a resolution, and refutes the arguments of the opposing side.

An argument answers the question why you favor or oppose the resolution.

Evidence defends and or explains your argument. Evidence may include the following: quotations, statistics/facts, and examples/anecdotes (be sure to include sources for these).

A refutation identifies an opponent's argument, then uses evidence or logic in an attempt to disprove it. (Yes, that's why debaters must take notes while others speak.)

A refutation may point out:
- misuse of evidence
- outdated evidence
- contradicting evidence
- an inappropriate authority
- leaps in logic:

   over-generalization
   "All tall people are good basketball players."

   no correlation between cause/effect
   "When I wear my green shirt, my team wins; therefore, my shirt causes the team to win."

   band-wagoning
   "Mom, everyone is going to the party, so you should let me go too."

   ad hominem (Don't attack the character of your opponent.)
   "My opponent is a man of severely limited intelligence."

   red-herring (changing the subject of the argument)
   "Do you believe school uniforms are important?"
   "Yes, but the quality of school lunches is really bad."

Sample/Example of Refutation

resolution: Resolved that the death penalty should be abolished in the United States.
argument: The death penalty does not deter crime.
evidence: According to Shirley Keller, author of *Murder Most Foul*, in 1998 there were fewer murders per capita in England, which does not have capital punishment, than in California, which does
refutation: It may be true that England had fewer murders per capita in 1998 than California (acknowledges argument), but there's nothing in the evidence to show that capital punishment or the absence of the death penalty had anything to do with the murder rate (notes a leap in logic—no correlation).

Appendix 4: Barriers to Listening

Listener _____

Contrast the barriers to listening that may occur in formal and informal listening situations. Join the audience to hear a formal speech (for example, a religious sermon, school board presentation, political debate) and record the types of barriers that affected (1) you and (2) other members of the audience. Contrast this situation to an informal setting when you are listening to a friend talk about something serious or important. Record the types of barriers that affected (1) you and (2) any other people present.

Formal Setting

Describe Situation _____

Barriers	Specific examples of what affected you	Specific examples of what affected others (if you could tell)
External Distractions		
Internal Distractions		
Listener's Desire to Speak		
Personal Biases		
Conflicting Demands		

Informal Setting

Describe Situation _____

Barriers	Specific examples of what affected you	Specific examples of what affected others (if you could tell)
External Distractions		
Internal Distractions		
Listener's Desire to Speak		
Personal Biases		
Conflicting Demands		

Apendix 5: Ten Keys to Effective Listening

These are positive guidelines to effective listening. They are at the heart of developing effective listening habits that will last a lifetime.

Keys to Effective Listening	A Passive Listener Will . . .	An Active Listener Will . . .
1. Find areas of interest	Tune out dry subjects	Ask, "What's in it for me?"
2. Judge content, not delivery	Tune out if delivery is poor	Judge content, skip over delivery errors
3. Wait to respond	Tend to enter into arguments	Not judge until comprehension is complete
4. Listen for ideas	Listen only for the facts	Listen for central themes, concepts, etc.
5. Be flexible	Take intensive notes using one system	Take fewer notes, using different systems, depending on situations
6. Work at listening; provide effective feedback	Show no energy output; fakes attention	Work hard; exhibit active body state
7. Resist distractions	Be easily distracted	Correct or avoid distractions; tolerate bad habits; concentrate
8. Exercise mind	Resist difficult material, seek light listening	Use heavier material to exercise mind
9. Keep mind open	React to emotional words easily	Interpret emotional words and get hung up on them
10. Capitalize on fact that thought is faster than speech	Tend to daydream when listening to slow speakers	Challenge; anticipate; mentally summarize; weigh the evidence; listen between the lines

Appendix 6: Video Terms

Actor   A person who appears on-camera in dramatic roles. The actor always portrays someone else.

Arc   The movement of the tripod and camera in a semicircular pattern.

Blocking   Carefully worked-out movement and actions by the talent and for all mobile video equipment used in a scene.

Camera Angles

High Angle   The shot is done by placing the camera above the object of interest and taking the shot looking down on it.

Low Angle   The shot is done by placing the camera below the object of interest and taking the shot looking up at it.

Reverse Angle/Over-the-Shoulder Shot (O/S)   Camera looks over the person's shoulder (shoulder and back of head included in shot) at the other person.

Line of Action   The technique that refers to always keeping the camera on the same side of the action.

Cant   Tilting the camera sideways

Cover Shot   A shot of the entire action. The shot a camera person goes to when uncertain what comes next.

Cut Away   A shot of an object or event that is peripherally connected with the overall event and that is neutral as to screen direction. Used to intercut between two shots in which the screen direction is reversed.

CU   Close Up   Object or any part of it seen at close range and framed tightly.

Cut   The instantaneous change from one shot (image) to another.

Cut In   Shots that are directly related to the central action.

Dolly   The camera and tripod move closer to and/or farther away from the subject.

Dub   The duplication of an electronic recording. The dub is always one generation away from the recording used for dubbing.

ECU   Extreme Close Up

ELS   Extreme Long Shot   Shows object from a great distance. Also called *Establishing Shot*, it shows the viewers what the whole looks like before they see a part.

Field Production   Any video production that happens outside the studio.

Flat Angle   An eye-level shot.

Full Shot   This shot fills the screen with the object being taped.

Generation   The number of dubs away from the original in analog recording. A first-generation dub is struck directly from the source tape. A second-generation tape is a dub of the first-generation dub (two steps away from the original tape), and so forth. The greater the number of generations, the greater the loss of quality.

Headroom   The space left between the top of the head and the upper screen edge.

Illustrative Music Video   The video is a literal description of the music in visual terms; in this video, the song is most important; the director is secondary.

Interpretive Music Video   The video uses images that relate indirectly to the music or the lyrics.

Into Frame   The subject comes into the shot to become the center of interest.

Jump Cut An image that jumps from one screen position to another during a cut.

Leadroom The space left in front of a laterally moving object or person.

Looking Room/Nose Room The space left in front of a person looking or pointing toward the edge of the screen.

MCU Medium Close Up Object seen at close range but framed loosely.

MS Medium Shot Object seen from a medium distance. Covers any framing between a long shot and a close up.

Out of Frame The subject of interest moves out of the shot.

Pan Horizontal turning of the camera from left to right or right to left while the tripod remains stationary.

Pedestal The up-and-down movement of the camera as the tripod is raised and lowered.

Performer A person who appears on camera in nondramatic shows. The performer does not assume someone else's character.

Pickup Pattern The territory around the microphone within which the mic can hear well.

Postproduction Any production activity that occurs after the production. Usually refers to either videotape editing or audio sweetening

Psychological Closure Mentally filling in missing visual information that will lead to a complete and stable configuration in the viewer's mind.

Preproduction Preparation of all production details.

Preroll To start a videotape and let it roll for a few seconds before it is put in the playback or record mode.

Production The actual activities in which an event is videotaped and/or televised.

Remote A production of a large, scheduled event done for live transmission or live-on-tape recording.

Remote Survey An inspection of the remote location by key production and engineering persons so that they can plan for the setup and use of production equipment. Also called site survey.

Rule of Thirds The principle that determines the most effective place on the screen to place the main character or object of interest.

Sequence An LS< MS< and CU of the same subject

Slate (1) To identify, verbally or visually, each videotaped take. (2) A little blackboard or whiteboard upon which essential production information is written, such as the title of the show, date, and scene and take numbers. It is recorded at the beginning of each videotaped take.

Storyboard A series of sketches of the key visualization points of an event, with the corresponding audio information given below each visualization.

Talent Collective name for all performers and actors who appear regularly in video.

Tilt The up-and-down movement of the camera while the tripod remains stationary.

Truck The lateral movement of the camera and tripod to the left or right.

Appendix 7: Warm Up Exercises

You can use the inflection lesson ("Did I Say That?"), enunciation exercise, and the tongue twisters as short lessons or as warm ups before a speaking assignment. You can also use them as remediation for students having difficulties with enunciation or pronunciation.

Enunciation Exercise

Students should practice sounding each set of words clearly enough so that a listener can identify which one is being said.

1. a nice house	an ice house
2. ice cream	I scream
3. night rate	nitrate
4. an aim	a name
5. lighthouse keeper	light housekeeper
6. maiden aim	maiden name
7. comic's trip	comic strip
8. icy	I see
9. eye strain	iced rain
	ice train
10. summer school	summer's cool
11. a narrow box	an arrow box
12. Nick's car	Nick's scar
13. a nice pick	an ice pick
14. clock stop	clock's top
15. heart throbbing	hearth robbing
16. green Nile	green isle
17. homemade	home aid
18. go for	gopher

Tongue Twisters

1. Rubber baby buggy bumpers.

2. She sells seashells by the seashore. If she sells seashells, the seashells are real seashells, I am sure.

3. Red leather, yellow leather.

4. The shell-shocked soldier shot his shotgun

5. He sawed six slick, slender, slippery, silver saplings.

6. A swan swam over the swell; swim, swan, swim. A swan swam back through the swell; well swum, swan!

7. Theophilus Thistle, the successful thistle sifter, in sifting a sieve full of unsifted thistles, thrust three thousand thistles through the thick of his thumb. See that thou in sifting a sieve full of unsifted thistles thrust not three thousand thistles through the thick of thy thumb.

8. A tree toad loved a she-toad that lived up in a tree. He was a three-toed tree toad, but a two-toad toad was she. The three-toed tree toad tried to win the she-toad's friendly nod, for the three-toed tree toad loved the ground that the two-toed tree toad trod!

9. A big black bear ate a big black bug.

10. The sixth sheik's sixth sheep's sick.

11. The seething sea ceaseth and thus the seething sea sufficeth us.

12. A tutor who tooted the flute
    Tried to tutor two tutors to toot.
    Said the two to the tutor
    Is it harder to toot, or
    To tutor two tooters to toot?

Appendix 8: Writing an Introduction

The first impression and the last impression are the speaker's chief concerns. As a speaker walks onto the platform and says the first sentence, the audience is forming its first impressions of that person as a speaker. If the audience reactions are favorable, obviously the task is easier. If their reactions are unfavorable, it will take hard work to transform unwilling listeners into an eager and attentive audience. The first impression is critical. Bliss Perry advised his students at Harvard University to "attract by the first phrase."

The **last step** in organizing a speech is developing the introduction. After the thesis has been clearly stated, after the main points have been logically organized and developed with interesting and relevant supporting materials, and after the conclusion has been planned, the speaker knows where the speech will take the audience. The introduction is an added part, which grabs the audience's attention.

- **Memorize your introduction:** Write your introduction out word-for-word. Starting off without faltering, stumbling, or repeating yourself will give the audience a good impression.

- **Get to the point:** Tie your introduction in with your subject and purpose as quickly and effectively as possible. Early ramblings may lose your listeners beyond recovery.

- **Show confidence:** Don't apologize for your preparation or for what you have to say. Explanations of this sort not only slow the beginning of a speech but they also tend to lose for you the respect and interest of the audience.

- **Open with short forceful sentences:** Short sentences have a directness that lends them punch. Long sentences, because they are harder to say and harder to follow, create an obstacle for both the passer and the receiver.

- **Make your opening inviting:** Let every listener feel that you're talking to him/her and that he/she will enjoy going along with you. Make him/her feel included and wanted in the experience you are going to share.

Key Methods of Introduction

A. Use a Startling Statement

Things that startle and shock us seize our attention. You may use statistics, little known facts, or unusual statements to catch the imagination and attention of your listeners.

Example: Content: Influenza Epidemic

Introduction: (Attention step) Before this week ends, one person in this room will be dead. (Transition sequence to thesis) There is some comfort in this number, though, because it represents only a statistical death. Records show one life in thirty. You may be lucky, but the death rate is tragic. There is, however, a way to stop this tragedy.

Thesis: By following three simple steps, we can reduce our chances of catching the flu.

B. Ask a Pertinent Question

A pertinent question *cannot* be answered "yes" or "no." To ask a pertinent question is a simple and sure way of getting the audience to think with you.

Example: Content: Vegetarianism

Introduction: (Attention step) When was the last time that you had a hamburger? What about a chicken burrito? Was it a week ago, two days, an hour? (Transition sequence to thesis) My answer would be two years. When I learned about the hazards to my body form eating meat, I became a vegetarian.

Thesis: The practices I follow as a vegetarian can lead to a longer life for me.

C. Open with a Strong Quotation

What someone else says is nearly always of interest to people, particularly if the person quoted is well known and respected. Quotations that are famous and easily recognized establish a feeling of familiarity with the subject and create in the audience a mood of acceptance toward the idea you intend to present. However, you must avoid triteness. Overused quotations may merely make the audience groan. Quotations should be easily understandable. While Shakespeare is often quoted, rarely can an audience understand the language in the early seconds of a speech. You may lose them.

Example: Individualism

Introduction: (Attention step) "Thousands of years ago, the first man discovered how to make fire. He was probably burned at the stake he had taught his brothers how to light. He was considered an evildoer who had dealt with a demon mankind dreaded. But, thereafter, man had fire to keep him warm, to cook their food, to light their food, and to light the caves. He had left them a gift they had not conceived and he had lifted darkness off the earth" (Transition sequence to thesis) This is the beginning of the story of individualism as told in *The Fountainhead* by Ayn Rand. Individualism has been the foundation of progress, but America is in danger because individualism is disappearing. To be effective, individualism has to be meaningful.

Thesis: We can choose effective, meaningful ways to be individualistic.

D. Use a Good Illustration

We all have curiosity about incidents, events, and people. Use an example or illustration that has human-interest value, and you'll put your audience in a listening mood. (It may be serious or humorous, real or fictional.)

Example (Fictional Illustration): Content: Home Accidents

Introduction: (Attention step) Douglas Keller was a promising young instructor in journalism at Duke University. At 8:15 on the night of October 15, he decided to take a bath. Because he wanted to finish reading an article while he was in the tub, and because the bathroom light was poorly located for good reading, he moved a standing

251

lamp from his bathroom and placed it beside the tub. Then he got into the tub, relaxed, and began to read. There was a glare from the light that bothered him a bit, so he reached up to shift the lamp slightly, and his hand came into contact with the socket. You know what happened, The doctor who arrived too late shook his head and said, "Far too many people die from accidents like this." (Transition sequence to thesis) Too often, home accidents are the result of careless behavior.

Thesis: By following basic home safety rules, home accidents can be avoided.

Example (Mildly Humorous Analogy): Content: Student Government
Introduction: (Attention step) I was discussing the dairy situation with a farmer friend recently and during the course of the conversation he remarked, "I have been experimenting with a cow. I've been using a toothbrush on the cow's teeth—now she's giving dental cream." (Transition sequence to thesis) Yes, people seem to experiment with everything these days. We have an interesting little experiment going on in our own little community, and, although it hasn't given any dental cream yet, it is providing us with cream of the crop in the way of civic improvement. I refer, of course, to the student government being conducted in our local high school.

Thesis: To understand this innovation clearly, we must analyze its origin, answer a few questions concerning its operation, and determine its value to the community.

Example (Real Life): Content: The Grading System
Introduction: (Attention step) Progress reports were handed out last Monday and what a reaction there was! The most frequent complaint I heard was "I didn't get a fair grade. The system is all wrong." (Transition sequence to thesis) These are comments to which I say, "Ridiculous!" I dare any of you to find a fairer grading system than we have here in our school now. What if you don't like the numbered ratings of 1, 2, 3, 4, and 5? All systems are basically the same. Teachers may give A's, B's, C's, D's, and F's; or they may rate us Excellent, Good, Fair, Passing, and Failures. Even if they used terms like Sensational, Magnificent, Stupendous, Colossal, and Super Colossal, results are the same.

Thesis: It isn't likely we'll get a better grading system than ours, and there are several reasons that support this position.

Introductions for Advanced Speakers
A. Refer to Your Physical Surroundings

Refer to your physical surroundings. You might refer to the temperature, the seating, the public address system situation shared by you and the audience. The more dramatic the condition, the more effective the reference.

Example: Content: School Building Program

Introduction: As you sit here today behind these scarred, poorly-shaped, uncomfortable desks; as you look at these cracked, patched, undecorated walls; as you breathe this hot, stuffy, and unchanged air, I want you to think with me about the need for a more adequate building program in our Cityville schools.

B. Refer to Other Speakers on the Program

This is a friendly and easy way to begin a speech. Listen to the speakers who procede you so that you can tie in their statements to your presentation.

Example: Content: Traffic Safety

Introduction: The previous speaker has given some detailed and dramatic examples about what is happening in the nation so far as accidents are concerned. The problem, though, is not only national. We are being seriously affected here in our town.

C. Refer to Your Audience

In this type of introduction, the speaker takes advantage of the self-interest of his listeners.

Example: A high school debater used this technique in a contest debate on the goals of education. He began, "Tonight, by actual count, there are twenty-seven members of our audience. Look at yourselves carefully, ladies and gentlemen. You represent that important minority in America that is still more interested in public education than in staying home this stormy night."

D. Refer to the Signficance of the Occasion

Don't abuse this method; many events are not really significant.

Example: A city-wide meeting has been called to dedicate a memorial to the former students of a local high school who had lost their lives in the last war. The principal was speaking to an audience that included most of the parents of these students. He began: "We are here tonight to pay tribute to the seventeen former students of our high school who lost their lives while serving in the armed forces for our country."

Appendix 9: Writing a Conclusion

The conclusion is a very important part of your speech because it is your last chance to attain the purpose of your speech. Consequently, while the tips on how to design a conclusion are relatively few, they are truly important.

The Major Purpose of the Conclusion is to emphasize the point of your speech, to bring your speech to a climax, and leave the audience remembering your speech.
Your conclusion should be presented in two sections:
- Review
- Memorable statement

Key Methods of Concluding
A. Summarize Your Points
In just a few words, present a brief, an abstract, an abridgment of the subject or viewpoint of your speech. A summary can be presented in either of two forms:
- Repeat word for word the same statement of your speech, subject or viewpoint that you presented in your preview of your speech.
- Rephrase your preview, stating the same content or idea, but in different wording. Some in an audience might tune out when they begin to hear the same words over again, but may listen alertly to the new, different statement.
  Examples:
  - Now you can understand my concern about the lack of controls on bicycle riders.
  - Those, then, are my reasons for urging you to vote for federal licensing of all boat operators.
  - Thus, I have built the case for eliminating billboards along our highways.

B. Repeat Your Main Points
In this structure of the conclusion, you repeat or rephrase the two to five main points you presented in the discussion part of your speech. Like a summary, a review of points can repeat them exactly as you stated them earlier in your speech, or you can rephrase them.
  Examples:
  - These, then, are the three keys to successful savings—*commitment, regularity, and growth.*
  - Thus we have examined what caused this tragic plane crash, and the effect it had on both the passengers and the company.
  - Such is the history of educational television—its decade of infancy, its decade of expansion, and now its decade of excellence.

- And so a writer progresses from thinking to doing, to evaluating, to finally mailing her manuscript.
- Four reasons, ladies and gentlemen, stand out as to why we must not let the incumbent mayor continue in office. He must not continue because he is dishonest. He must not continue because he is prejudiced. He must not continue because he is hard to work with. And he must not continue because he is out of date.

  Note the parallel construction, used in the last two examples, about the writer and the mayor; such repetitive phrasing is often particularly effective in the conclusion.

C. Combine a Summary with a Repetition

Many speakers find it most effective to combine those last two techniques to present both a summary of the main subject or idea of their speeches, and a repeat of the main points. These examples illustrate both repeating and rephrasing, and also the use of parallel construction, to emphasize, to add interest, and to make points more memorable.

Examples:
- Those, then, are the three reasons that have led me to invest in mutual funds. First, they provide safety in diversity; second, they provide participation in the growth of our nation's industry; and third, they provide me with money.
- Think again of our candidate's background—her training, her experience, and her achievements. Then, certainly, you'd vote for her with enthusiasm.

D. Present a Memorable Statement

For your memorable statement you can select from any of the eleven techniques for getting the attention of your audience in the introduction of your speech.

1. Ask a question.
2. State an unusual fact.
3. Give an illustration, example or story.
4. Present a quotation.
5. Refer to a historic event.
6. Tell a joke.
7. Use a gimmick.
8. Point to common relationships, beliefs, interests, or opinions.
9. Refer to the occasion, purpose of the meeting, audience, a local event, or some other part of the program.
10. Compliment the audience.
11. Point out the importance of the subject to the audience.

In using these in the conclusion, apply the same general guides that you learned for using them in your introduction.

E. Return to the Theme of Your Attention-Getter

It is particularly effective in closing a speech to present again the same story, incident, quotation, joke, etc., that you used as your attention-getter, but now with a different ending, or an additional line, or perhaps another insight or explanation.

F. Look to the Future

Both President John F. Kennedy and his brother Robert often closed many of their speeches with these words by poet Robert Browning: "Some men see things the way they are, and ask, 'Why?' I dare to dream of things that never were, and ask, 'Why not?'" Pointing to the future extends to your audience the invitation to consider, explore, and think further about your subject. This is in contrast to the other techniques for a memorable statement, which at times may tend to close the subject, with your concluding remarks perhaps ending your listener's thinking.

Example:

- Thus we have seen the past and the present of our problems of mass transportation. But what of the future? Is it in your hands, ladies and gentlemen? You, as our city council, can write the future of mass transportation through the vote you are now about to cast. May your decision be based not on a misty look at the past, not on a blurred glance at the present. But rather, may your decision be based on a clear vision of our future.

G. Call for Action

The purpose of a speech to persuade is, of course, to get action—to move the audience to buy, join, vote, march. Consequently, the memorable statement for a sales talk is usually an appeal for action. A plentiful source of examples for such speech conclusions is television commercials.

- So next time you're in your grocery store, pick up a package of . . .
- Call now to get your special invitation—call this number, call now!!
- Now that you've just seen how truly fast this spray works, show your family how fast you can get rid of bugs by going out right now to buy a can for your home.

Of course, other types of speeches, too, present an appeal for action—the minister spurring his congregation to attend a special meeting, the politician seeking your vote, the teacher urging you to study. Make an appeal for action when action is needed—but make it a realistic appeal, one that can be fulfilled.

H. Attention-Getting Criteria

Remember this acronym as the criteria for a good attention-getter for your introductions and conclusions: RIPS. It will spark in your mind the following key words:

Relevant

Involves the Audience

Positive thinking by audience

Stimulates audience

Things to Avoid in Your Conclusion

Don't merely stop at the end of your material: It is the conclusion, that brings together all that you've presented. Therefore, don't simply present your final point with its last bit of data and then stop. Rather, bring coherence through a well-worded conclusion.

- **Don't apologize:** "So that's about it, and I'm really sorry I didn't have all the figures for that budget, but there wasn't time, and I hope you kinda get the idea. If you have questions I could try to answer them." Don't reveal lack of preparation by verbalizing it. The damage has already been done.

- **Don't stretch it out:** The rambling, wandering, I-don't-know-when-to-sit-down speaker is one of the most distasteful people to have to listen to.
  - Get to your point.
  - Summarize specific, precise points.
  - Finish with something we'll remember.
  - Finish! Please!

- **Don't introduce new points:** If, in fact, a really critical point comes up that you did overlook, try to be polished enough as a speaker to ease into the point smoothly. This may happen following a question-and-answer period, in which a question from the audience might uncover a basic point that you had not yet presented. You might work it into your planned conclusion by wording it so that the new point seems to have unity and a relationship with the rest of your speech.

- **Don't say, "And one thing more I wanted to say ...":** This point is an extension, an example, in effect, of the one above. But it gets its own paragraph because that unpleasant phrase is used so often and is so distasteful.

- **Don't pack up early:** Stay up before the audience, presenting your ideas, and not giving them the idea that you've quit thinking about your subject by picking up your notes, putting them in your pocket, starting toward your seat, or otherwise deserting your spot before the audience, until you're finished speaking.

- **Don't continue to speak as you leave the lectern: Stay before that audience, maintaining contact, until your final words are out. Then, take a slight pause, and move out.**

Appendix 10: Sample Persuasive Speech with MLA Documentation

The following speech was written by the 2003 California State Champion in Oratory. It is printed here for the purpose of illustrating the use of MLA documentation in a persuasive speech.

Tin-Yun Ho
Bellarmine College Preparatory
3 February 2003

Memories

Jury duty. A phrase that evokes passionate displays of patriotism like none other. From our almost universal response to that noble call of duty, the true character of an American citizen is revealed. "Well your honor, I can't serve because I'm biased! I already know he's guilty. I'm a professional psychic!" "Sir, that is not a legitimate reason for . . ." "But I can tell he's guilty! Look at him, fox eyes, crooked nose, oily black toupee . . ." "Sir, you're describing the lawyer." Or better yet, don't even show up to court! Just throw away the jury summons, or do it in style like the man from Connecticut, who, according to Ananova News, took the jury summons, used it as toilet paper, and sent it back to the judge. When questioned, he replied, "Jury Duty . . . STINKS!" (Ananova News). You may laugh, but the underlying attitudes these stories reveal are widespread. For according to sociologist Morris Janowitz, Americans expect to be given a trial by jury, but we don't want to serve on one (8). We're freeloaders. Pirates, Buccaneers. We expect the community to give us rights, privileges, all sorts of goods. But we don't expect to give anything in return.

We can see this mindset in Santa Monica, California, where men were found dealing drugs in women's public restrooms. Obviously, the City Council didn't like this, so they prohibited both men and women from using the opposite sex's facilities. The drug sales ceased. However, a local activist, Gloria Allred, instantly protested. To her, this ordinance was a violation of a woman's right to urinate in any public facility, at any time.

[Margin note: Documentation of paraphrased material from the Internet, with no author.]

[Margin note: Author cited in text; need only page number.]

As she stated, "This is the first step down a long dark road of restricting women's rights" (Etzioni, *Spirit* 5). The Rosa Parks of the 21st century: "I refuse to leave my bathroom!" You see, Allred was so obsessed with freedom that she forgot something essential. That maybe some kids don't want to be abused by drug dealers in the bathroom. That just maybe, some parents wouldn't like it either. Allred forgot common decency. Care for others around her. And she is not the only one.

> Documentation of directly quoted material from one of two sources by the same author.

When the Foundation of People for the American Way did a survey on what made America special, the response was unanimous. One said "individualism" (*People* 9). Another said, "the right to do whatever you want" (11) another said "no limits" (11). Freedom, That's what we call it. Every genuine American knows how to use that word in a punch line, and if you're like Bush, it's probably the only word you know, besides "evil" and "greater evil" ("*Axis of Evil*".) In other words, it's the cheapest word in the American dictionary. For as American Way concluded in its report, the citizens of America "fail to grasp the other half of the democratic equation" (15). That of duty and responsibility.

> Quotations run in with text. Documentation of first uses title, those that follow use page only, if from the same source.

It's the kind of mentality that makes two-thirds of Americans report that they don't like the way the government runs, but at the same time, according to Roper Political Trends, we're 42 percent less likely to serve in a political organization, 42 percent less likely to work for a political cause (Putnam 45), and according to sociologist Russel Dalton, are the second most apathetic democratic population in the world (Dalton 74). Well Fine. Al Gore isn't exactly the most motivational speaker. Kinda more like a bad extemper. Well . . . kinda like a good one too. But have we taken this too far?

> Documentation of paraphrased statistical information from single sources, some with single authors.

In America today, according to the Center of Popular Economics, over 44 percent of divorced fathers refuse to pay for the care of their own children (Albeda 50). Elsewhere, men and women burn flags in front of veterans of war, and then invoke the first amendment to protect themselves. There's a corporation for every letter of the alphabet that has used its power to swindle the public. And finally, despite the fact that, according to Time magazine, 9 out of 10 nursing homes are inadequately staffed or have committed multiple health violations (Service 3), we put 1.7 million of our own parents into their

> Documentation of paraphrased information from a pamphlet by a single author.

hands. As a result, 3,500 of our elderly die from nursing home abuse and neglect each year (Thompson 45). Neglect doesn't happen overnight! When all this happened, where were we?

However, none of this comes close to the greatest fault of our society. I encountered it on my way home from school. I was in the city, lined up behind about 6 cars at an intersection, waiting for the light to change. On the side of the road, a man who had been sitting stood up. He knocked on each window, held up a placard asking for money, and then mouthed the word "please." And as I watched, he went to every single car window in front of me, and no one moved. And when he came to my window, I closed it, locked the door, and straight ahead, pretending not to see him. I never took that road again.

According to the U.S. census bureau, about 36 million Americans live in poverty (U.S. Census Bureau). In France, these people are called *les excludes* (*Leo* 17). The excluded. In the Old Testament, the root word for "the poor" is more rightfully translated as "the oppressed" (Hanks). But what do we call them? Hobos. Bums. Welfare queens. The average industrialized nation spends 30% of the national budget on welfare for the poor (Etzioni, "*How to . . .*" 25). We spend half as much. According to sociologist Robert Putnam, our charitable giving, already one of the lowest in the Western world, has decreased by 30 percent since the 1960s (124). And finally, even when, according to the Children's Defense Fund, every 43 seconds a child is born into poverty so extreme that their mental development is at risk (Children's Defense Fund 8), President Bush decides to give my twelve-year-old sister a $200 tax rebate. Thanks. We really needed it. Maybe now she can pay her phone bill. Ladies and Gentlemen, it's as if every window were closed, every door locked. Is this what we've come to? Is this who we are?

Two hundred years ago, James Madison, the chief architect of the Constitution, stated, "I go on this great republican principle, that the people of America will have the virtue and the intelligence . . . to fight for the [common good], themselves . . ." (*Bellah* 253). With that undying faith in us, James Madison forcibly turned America into a democracy and forged the Bill of Rights, the greatest article of freedom in the world. But what have we done with that freedom? We've turned it into the freedom to ignore

Documentation of directly quoted material from one of two sources, by the same author.

Author cited in text; need only page number

our families, shun that community, and leave children sleeping in the streets. The freedom to let our nation fall apart. Is this what James Madison fought for? Is this what Martin Luther King dreamed of? Is this what Joseph Farrely, firefighter for New York's Division 1 battalion, died for?

You see, at the heart of their struggles was a different conception of freedom. It wasn't the freedom to just be yourself, be natural, and do whatever you feel like doing, because then we'd also be free to give oratories naked and dance like Janet Reno . . . at the same time! Freedom in that sense is foolish and meaningless. Rather, to them, freedom was as simple as this:

I am third in line to sign the Declaration of Independence. Within two years, my son will be dead and I will be hanged for treason. I am an Irish refugee from my famine-stricken homeland, seeing the Statue of Liberty for the first time. I am a Nisei, a Japanese man in an internment camp, signing up to fight for the country that took everything I have. I'm walking on the moon. The success and shame, hopes and fears of ten thousand years flow through my veins, pushing me inexorably towards my future. I am not just me, I am so much more. And I alone realize that the whole history of the world can be changed by what I do. This is the kind of freedom I inherited. The greatest gift I ever received from mankind. But I refuse to believe that I am the only one that matters. That this gift is for my use and my use only. Because if Neil Armstrong only took one small step for himself, he'd be stepping into one lonely place, no matter how high, how grand. So instead, I go by the great Christian motto, that "to whomsoever much is given of him, much is to be expected" (The Holy Bible, Luke 12.48). And I am proud to stand ready, at the call of duty.

> Citing the Bible is done by citing the version used, followed by the book, chapter and verse.

Works Cited

Albeda, Randy. *The War on the Poor*. New York: New Press, 1996.

Ananova News. "Man uses jury summons as toilet paper and sends it back." Retrieved 22 Aug. 2002. <http://www.ananova.com/news/story/sm_655538.html >.

Bellah, Robert N. *Habits of the Heart*. Berkeley: University of California Press, 1996.

Children's Defense Fund. "State of Children in America's Union." 2002 <http://www.childrensdefense.org/pdf/minigreenbook.pdf. >

Dalton, Russell. *Citizen Politics*. Chatham: Chatham House, 1996.

Etzioni, Amitai, "How to Make a Humane Market." *New Statesman*. November 20, 1998: 25–7.

_____. *The Spirit of Community*. New York: Crown Publishers, 1993.

Hanks, Tom, "Why People are Poor." The American Lutheran Church: Hunger Program Minneapolis.

Janowitz, Morris. *The Reconstruction of Patriotism*. Chicago: University of Chicago Press, 1983.

Leo, John. "Community and Personal Duty" *U.S. News & World Report*. January 28, 1991: 17.

People of the American Way. *Democracy's Next Generation*. Washington: People for the American Way, 1989.

Putnam, Robert D. *Bowling Alone* New York: Simon and Schuster, 2000.

Service Employees International Union. "A Crisis of Care." California, April 2001.

The Holy Bible, New International Version. Grand Rapids: Zondervan, 1992.

Thompson, Mark, "Fatal Neglect," *Time* Magazine. October 27, 1997.

U.S. Census Bureau. "Poverty 2001" Retrieved 12 December 2002. <http://www.census.gov/hhes/poverty/poverty01/r&dtable6.html.>

Callout boxes: Title one inch from top; double space to first entry. Entries arranged alphabetically. Internet source includes date of access. Shows second source by Etzioni, alphabetized by title. Unsigned Internet source.

Index of Lesson Plans

Index of Activity and Resource Sheets